COACHING PERSPECTIVES VIII

Center for Coaching Certification

Cathy Liska

Ruth Pearce

Wayne L. Anderson

Shelley Young Thompkins

Lisa Foster

Wilhelmina Parker

Melissa Tyler Todd

Rachel Coucoulas

Necie Black

Kristen Hess-Winters

Renee Hutcherson Lucier

Chārutā AhMaiua

Dear Reader,

The group of Certified Professional and Master Coaches included here have shared their journey through training and now writing. Each coach author writing a chapter offers amazing expertise. Working with them is a great privilege.

The content of each chapter is a unique read of 15 to 20 minutes; after that you will want to read it again to deepen awareness of the insights.

Whether you are a coach or reading this to learn from the expertise of these coaches, enjoy the tips, processes, and wisdom.

Kindly let us know how we can be helpful.

Sincerely,

Cathy Liska
Guide from the Side®
Center for Coaching Certification

CENTER FOR COACHING CERTIFICATION

www.CoachCert.com

Info@CoachCert.com

800-350-1678

MISSION:
Enhance your coach training experience with
quality, professionalism, and support.

VISION:
A high-quality, ethical norm throughout the coaching
profession achieved through leadership by example.

For coaches,
those thinking about becoming a coach,
and those who receive coaching.

Table of Contents

Tools, Techniques, Questions, and Dialogue
Cathy Liska

Simple insight for new coaches on tools, techniques, questions, and processes is told through a client created by blending multiple clients with information changed to protect privacy.

About the Client

After being downsized or rightsized with several different companies, Katrina was discouraged. She was divorced, in her late forties, living in a caretaker's room on an estate in exchange for watching the house, and completely unsure of her next steps.

A friend recommended coaching and Katrina called.

Starting the Coaching Relationship

Ensuring that coaching made sense for Katrina and that I was a good match started with an introductory session. Katrina had the opportunity to experience coaching and determine her own comfort level both with me and with the coaching process. When the session was complete, Katrina shared that it was very interesting to her that instead of telling her what to do, I asked her what she wants and her thoughts on moving forward.

1

Because Katrina and I both determined we were a good match, we moved into reviewing the Code of Ethics and Coaching Agreement. Given Katrina's circumstances, we chose to work together with Katrina paying a minimal fee until she was employed again. In addition to coaching, we discussed possible training and/or consulting as additional service options.

In the introductory session, Katrina identified her immediate focus as building her confidence and figuring out her direction. Because of this, we explored how to start working together.

Sample extracts from the conversation:

Coach: One of the choices in terms of how we work together is a focus on finding a job. An alternative is starting with a big picture exploration of what you want in all areas of your life and then moving into what you want to work on with you choosing when to focus on each goal. Another option is an assessment.

Katrina: I don't feel ready to just get a job for the sake of a job, and I want to figure things out, so the big picture exploration seems like it will help. I really want a sounding board to help me figure out what is most important.

Coach: Seems you relaxed into the idea – is that right?

Katrina: Yeah – that is how I feel.

FIRST PRIORITY: CONFIDENCE

During the opening session as Katrina explored what she wanted, she used self-limiting language. She doubted her ability to achieve all she wanted. Katrina, like so many of us have been, was at a time in her life where her confidence was low. Because of this, we explored creating a tool to support her confidence, create a sense of positive empowerment, and keep her focused on moving toward her goals.

The tool used for Katrina was her personal story affirming what she wanted. This means her goals in her words written as a story in the present tense describing her being on track for achieving her goals. The story used Katrina's positive and proactive language (consistently asked for throughout the opening session) and her specific goals. We scheduled time for Katrina to hear her story read to her as a guided visualization exercise. Katrina shared that the first time she listened she was resistant to it becoming real. After hearing it multiple times she said she began accepting the possibility.

Sample extracts from the opening conversation:

Coach: Katrina the time today is for you to explore what you want in all different areas of your life. How are you feeling?

Katrina: Excited and nervous. I am ready though.

Coach: This time is your time and you are in the driver's seat.

This time is your time and you are in the driver's seat.

Katrina: Thank you.

Sample extracts from the end of opening conversation:

Coach: What are your insights from what you shared?

Katrina: Some of these things are very important and I forgot about them. This really has me thinking about my priorities.

Coach: What are you thinking about your priorities?

Katrina: I want to do some more thinking about how I use my time and what I focus on. I want to think about a job that gives me time for my life too. I want to let this all sink in.

Sample extracts from the second coaching session:

Coach: What have you been thinking about since the last session?

Katrina: I have been day dreaming and questioning what matters and really thinking through what I discovered about my goals and what is most important.

Coach: What did you discover?

Katrina: That I say family and friends are a priority and then I put all my time into a job. I want to have a way of reminding myself. I want to build my confidence and set boundaries.

Coach: That sounds like it means a lot to you – is that correct?

Katrina: Yes. Reminding myself and affirming myself.

Coach: One tool for building confidence and reminding yourself to stay focused on your goals is your story based on your goals written the way you said it. How do you feel about the idea?

Katrina: That sounds interesting – a little uncomfortable – and I am ready for something different.

SECOND PRIORITY: BEING INTENTIONAL ABOUT CAREER

After Katrina had her story and started using it, she wanted to move forward with her focus on career. She knew she wanted a job that gave her time for other things too. She was still working through exactly what type of job she wanted to pursue.

In talking possible approaches with Katrina, she decided she wanted to start by working through what she liked doing at work, her skills, and job possibilities. We discussed co-creating lists for ranking or defining, utilizing a series of questions on changing or choosing a career, and the Guide from the Side® game that included choosing and defining values, plus prioritizing relationships, time, money, and goals.

Coach: Some clients find it helpful to list skills, jobs, or values, etc. and then either prioritize or self-evaluate.   What seems helpful for you?

Katrina: Hm.   I think a list of skills will help.   Defining my values feels like a good next step.   Then possible jobs because that will help me prioritize.

Coach: Great – you want to start with your skills – is that correct?

Katrina: Yes.   Okay, I am good at…

Coach: Katrina great job!

Katrina: Thanks.   It was helpful.

After she developed her list, for deeper insight we talked about assessments.

Coach: An additional tool is assessments.   Assessments are validated instruments available in a variety of areas.   For example, there are assessments that identify behavior style, motivational style, thinking style, Emotional IQ, and learning styles as well as areas for professional growth.   In addition to a deeper awareness for yourself, assessments provide insight on strengths or areas to develop.   What are your thoughts?

Katrina: I have wanted to take the Emotional IQ assessment because sometimes I am challenged by managing my own reactions and knowing how to react to others.

Coach: For the assessment I will send you a link, login and respond to the questions.   We will review the results together in a coaching session, and then I will send you your full report.

Katrina: That makes sense.   When will you send the link?

Coach: That will take just a few minutes.   When do you want to schedule time to review the results?

Katrina: Sometime next week.

When Katrina had finished answering the questions, the report came in.   As coach, preparing for the coaching session includes reviewing the information on the assessment dashboard that explains the report, reviewing the report itself, and being intentional planning for the coaching session.   Specifically, I like to set up an email or two with a generic diagram or checklist explaining the information we will review together.   Being ready for a screen share makes it easier to review the report together. Use powerful coaching questions before, during, and after - here are a few examples to get you started:

Before

- How are you feeling about today's conversation?
- What are your thoughts about what we will review?
- What are your questions on how the report is organized?

During

- As you review your results in each section, talk out loud about what you see, think, and feel.
- What are you learning about yourself?
- What are you liking?
- What areas you want to develop further?
- What insights does this provide?
- What are your opportunities for shifting things?
- What are the benefits of this awareness?
- How do you want to use what you are learning?
- What additional thinking or reflecting will you do?
- What do you want to be asked the next time we meet?

After

- What are your thoughts since we last met and discussed your assessment?
- What are you learning about your situation?
- What are you learning about yourself?
- How is this helping you?
- What do you want to adjust?
- How will you maximize the awareness?

After reviewing the assessment, Katrina's next step was listing and ranking possible jobs. This started with brainstorming, moved to free online assessments for identifying jobs, and expanded to Katrina researching plus asking friends for suggestions. After developing the list, I supported Katrina in grouping the types of jobs, then listing likes and dislikes of the groups, and finally prioritizing based on her interests.

With the heightened awareness gained from the lists, self-evaluation, assessments, and prioritizing job possibilities, the focus for Katrina moved to her resume and job search. Because we had talked about the possibility of also scheduling training or consulting, I asked Katrina her thoughts. Katrina felt comfortable with writing a resume; she wanted consulting on the resume when it was ready. Katrina decided that once she began her search, skills training was an option if it applied.

Coach: How are you feeling about what you are learning?

How are you feeling about what you are learning?

Katrina: This has been great – I feel like I am clear on what is important and what I want to be doing.

Coach: Excellent – way to go! When you say clear, what does that mean?

Katrina: Well, when we started my thoughts were all over the place. I could easily have gotten a job to have a job and now I am going to look for a job I want. It feels like I am moving in the right direction. I feel like the work we did is preparing me for the long-term and I like that.

Coach: What is does moving in the right direction mean for you?

Katrina: It is important to do work that I am interested in – and I want it to feel like what I do matters. I want to find a job that supports a more balanced life. Instead of rushing back to the corporate world I am going to really be smart about which companies are appealing for me. It is important that balance is a priority and that they know it. I realize it is important to take care of myself so that when I am working I am focused and at home I can relax. I feel like I am in a good place now and ready to move forward.

Coach: Wonderful – seems you have been reflecting. Even your tone of voice is different now compared to when we started.

Katrina: Yeah – I guess my tone is different because how I feel is different – like we discussed. I feel good about my job search and I am ready.

Coach: Sounds like you have ideas for your job search too. What do you want to focus on now?

Katrina: Well, I am ready to work on my resume.   Then we can plan my job search.

RESUME

In setting up the coaching relationship, the option for training or consulting in addition to coaching was discussed.   For her resume, Katrina wanted to schedule consulting.   This meant she provided a copy of her updated resume and asked for help. During the consulting process, coaching questions were used. Here are a few examples:

- What are your significant measurable successes?
- How do you stand out from other candidates?
- What do you want to highlight for your ideal job?
- What are the expectations of an employer?
- What will your ideal employer want to see?
- How does this resume demonstrate your ability to do the job?
- How will an employer know you will fit their culture?
- What will be a value-add for an employer?

With the resume fine-tuned, the next step Katrina chose was to ensure social media profiles were up to date and consistent. Additionally, it was important for Katrina to feel comfortable with a potential employer seeing everything she had online. Coaching questions again helped during the consulting session:

- Which pictures are you comfortable with anyone seeing?
- Which elements of your resume do you want included?
- What narrative do you want to add?
- What interests do you want included?

JOB SEARCH

When Katrina felt good about her resume and social media profiles, she was ready to begin her job search.

During the coaching session, we brainstormed so Katrina had a list of options:
- Job Boards
- Identifying companies of interest and inquiring
- Informational interviews
- Networking
- Unsolicited applications
- Respond to job postings

Katrina next worked on her action plan. Her steps included:
- Post resume on selected job boards
- Invest an hour each day researching companies online
- Submit one inquiry each day to a company of interest
- Ask for one informational interview each week
- List people in her network and sort as referrals or contacts within a company of interest

- Call or email two people in her network each week
- Submit one unsolicited resume each week
- Respond to two job postings each week

Coach: Great work Katrina – seems you are focused, and that you have great ideas.

Katrina: Yes. Now that I am ready, I am diving in and plan to make finding my ideal job my full-time job.

Coach: How does that commitment feel?

Katrina: Good. I feel energized. I feel like I have a purpose. I am excited and nervous too. I am ready to go.

DECISION TIME

Within three weeks of her dedicated efforts to find a job, Katrina received two offers. She wanted to talk through both offers and decide which to accept.

Examples of coaching questions to help Katrina decide:
- What are the pros of offer A?
- What are the cons of offer A?
- What are the pros of offer B?
- What are the cons of offer B?

- How significant is each pro and con?
- What are the short-term considerations?
- What are the long-term considerations?
- How does offer A fit with your priorities?
- How does offer B fit with your priorities?
- What do you like least about each option?
- What do you like most about each option?
- What are the implications for others in your life with each offer?
- What are the implications for your self-care with each offer?
- Five years from now, what do you want to look back on?
- How do you want to decide?

Thinking about and answering the questions helped Katrina consider her options and identify the best fit. When she decided which she wanted, she sounded happy and confident.

Coach: The way you said that sounds happy – a shift in your energy. You sound confident. What are you experiencing?

> *– a shift in your energy... What are you experiencing?*

Katrina: Yeah – I am happy and knowing what I am doing feels right so I see that as the confidence. This feels good.

Coach: Katrina way to go – you are openly considering everything, thinking it through, and making your choice.

Katrina: The questions help and having this time to think and talk is good. I feel like I am being smart about this job search.

NEGOTIATING THE OFFER

After working through the possibilities and making her decision, Katrina wanted to work on negotiating her best deal. We discussed coaching versus training versus consulting. Katrina felt she had the book knowledge on negotiating and opted to stay engaged with coaching.

Coach: What does your research tell you about this offer?

Katrina: For the position it seems to be just above the low end. I think that with my experience it is fair to ask for more.

Coach: When asking for more, how will you make your case?

Katrina: Note the research, highlight my experience, and define the benefits for them in paying me more.

Next on Katrina's list was planning how to turn the second offer down gracefully. Starting with questions helped Katrina organize the information and write several responses to consider.

- What do you appreciate most about the offer you are turning down?

- What do you appreciate most about the people you interacted with?
- What do you appreciate about the company?
- What is your level of interest in reconnecting in the future?
- What will they notice in a letter?
- What is important for you to express?

During the coaching session we co-created a letter and several alternatives. Katrina opted to sit with what was developed and then mail the letter within one day.

DEVELOPING WORKPLACE STRATEGIES

Katrina's first day in her new job was fast approaching and she wanted to work on how she was going to set herself up for success. In talking through how to work on this together, Katrina decided that identifying the stages for starting and engaging was the first step. Next was to think through what each stage meant to her and what she wanted to be aware of as she was in that stage. Finally, Katrina wanted to define specific actions for each stage. The stages and points of awareness she developed during the coaching included:

- Preparation – in preparing for work, Katrina wanted to identify who she was going to interact with and plan her logistics such as office and schedule.

- Clarity about Role and Expectations – Katrina wanted to review her job description, make notes on anything that was unclear to plan learning opportunities, and get the specifics on expectations.

- Designing Impact – once she knew the expectations, Katrina wanted to figure out how to meet and exceed them. She wanted to identify where she was going to make the greatest impact.

- Reflecting – Katrina wanted to plan time to intentionally reflect on the people, culture, and work to identify what was going well and where she wanted to adjust.

- Understanding the Company – Katrina wanted to take the time to talk to colleagues about the company history, the culture, the vision for the future, company values, and how everyone fit in the big picture.

- Questions – Katrina planned to make a list of questions to ask her boss, her colleagues, and her direct reports.

- Priorities – Katrina wanted to plan time after a month on the job to evaluate her priorities.

- Leadership Style – Katrina wanted to plan a review of her leadership style plus strategize how she wanted to enhance her effectiveness.

- Building the Team – Katrina wanted to chart her team including their personalities, strengths, goals, and how to most effectively empower each of them.

- Getting Results – Katrina wanted to plan regular reviews of her work, evaluate her results, and to set goals plus design strategies moving forward.

Coach: Great job Katrina.   How do you feel about your list and points of awareness?

Katrina: It feels solid.   It covers all the key areas and is really going to help me as I adjust.   I feel like I have things to reflect on and direction for what to do next.   After all, I want to make a good impression.

> *I feel like I have things to reflect on ...*

Coach: How do you want to be perceived as you adjust?

Katrina: I want to be seen as knowledgeable, engaged, a team player, effective, and a great boss.

Coach: How will you know when you achieve this?

Katrina: People on my team will seek me out for input.   My team will also come to talk when they are facing challenges. They will know they can be honest about personal things affecting them too.   Most importantly, they will know they can make decisions and act.

Coach: What will you say and do to create that?

Katrina: I will identify their personal styles and be aware of that when we talk.   I will ask them to help me get to know them.   I will share my goals and what kind of a leader I want to be and ask for their input.   I will ask them for their goals and how I can help them achieve what they want.

Coach: Seems you have been thinking about this Katrina.

Katrina: Yes.   I was thinking about what I liked and didn't like at my last job.   I thought about everything we discussed for my ideal job.   I reviewed what we discussed when I chose this job. The relationships with people make the biggest impact on my success, so I included that awareness in my decision.

Coach: How do you want to acknowledge yourself for this work and awareness?

Katrina: I hadn't thought about that.   I do want to acknowledge myself.   It will help me be confident when I start, and it will keep me focused too.   Well, I am going to take a day this weekend before I start and do some of my favorite things!   I am going for a long walk.   I will even schedule a massage.   I am going to watch a good movie.   This sounds good!

Coach: You seem excited and content – is that right?

Katrina: Absolutely!

Coach: Katrina you also wanted to plan your action steps.   Are you ready for that now?

Katrina: Yes!   Let's take each stage and list what I will do.

DESIGNING A CAREER PATH

After Katrina had been working for 4 months, she was ready to start thinking through her career path with the company. During the coaching session, we explored the elements for planning her career path and how she defined each:

- Value – what unique value I bring to the company.
- Strengths and Weaknesses – how to maximize my strengths and how to manage my weaknesses.
- Goals – what I want to accomplish at work.
- Timeline – put goals on a timeline that encompasses the short term and on out using a big picture approach for the long term.
- Network – who is in my network, how I help them, what I can ask them for help on.
- Strategies – what my approach will be to achieve goals and advance to the next level on the job.

Next, I asked Katrina about her action plan for each of the elements.   She defined action steps that involved doing as well as actions that focused on thinking, reflecting, and being aware.

BUILDING A LIFE

After six months on the job, Katrina was ready to start thinking about planning for other areas of her life. She chose to focus on budgeting, finding a new home, building relationships, wellness, and self-care.

For the session on budgeting, Katrina wanted to write a budget plus explore technologies for managing it. She wanted to work through amounts for everything. We talked options and Katrina chose to start simple and use the Excel tool (available on the coach login page). As we went through what she spent, I asked her questions to expand her thinking.

- Share your thinking on the amount.
- What level of flexibility do you want with your budget?
- How will you budget for the future?

When Katrina chose to talk about finding a home, I asked questions to help explore considerations and choose priorities.

- What are your considerations in choosing a home?
- What is important to you in a home?
- Where do you want to live?
- What features do you want?
- What are deal breakers?
- What are your deciding factors?
- What is your timeline?

What are your deciding factors?

21

For the session when Katrina wanted to focus on relationships, she separated her relationships into the categories of workplace, neighborhood, friends, and family. She listed people in each category. I asked her about time, activities, and how she wanted to be in each of the relationships.

- What types of relationships are you focused on?
- Who are the people in your life now?
- Who else do you want in your life?
- How much time do you want with them?
- What do you want to do with them?
- How do you want to treat them?
- How do you want to feel when you are with them?

Wellness and self-care came up for Katrina. We talked about ways to approach the topics. Katrina wanted to identify what she did currently for herself, what she wanted to start doing again, how to be aware of her self-care, and how to ensure she kept it a priority.

- What do you do now that is taking care of you?
- What feels good for you?
- What amount of time is right for you to dedicate to yourself?
- What activities are helpful to you?
- What are your thoughts about time for reflection?
- What is important about self-care?
- What might get in the way?
- How will you ensure you do manage your self-care?

- What support will help you?
- What resources will help you?
- How will you plan your self-care?

Then I asked Katrina if she was ready to talk about wellness and she said yes.

- What is wellness for you?
- What do you want to include for your wellness?
- What is your knowledge base?
- What are your sources of information?
- What helps you stay on track?
- What level of activity or exercise do you want?
- How detailed do you want your eating plan to be?
- What motivates you?

One of the great things about coaching is that the process works with or without subject matter expertise because the client is in charge of choosing the focus and approach, and of finding their answer. The coach asks questions.

> *...the process works with or without subject matter expertise because the client is in charge of choosing the focus and approach, and of finding their answer.*

REFLECTION

In the example shared here, the client moved through many phases and worked in many areas of their life. While each client is different in terms of how many things are covered in coaching, taking time to reflect on what they accomplished, and their coaching experience adds value.

- How are you feeling about your coaching experience?

- What have you accomplished?

- What is the meaning of your progress and successes?

- What have you learned?

- What are your insights?

- How did coaching help?

- How will you continue to build on your achievements?

- How will you use the coaching process after coaching?

- How will you decide when to reengage with a coach?

Coaching is a privilege because of the trust clients have in our care of them and their information. It is a privilege because we get to be partners for part of their journey. It is a privilege because we celebrate their progress and success with them. It is a privilege because we learn in the process.

> *Coaching is a privilege because of the trust clients have in our care of them and their information.*

Cathy Liska is founder and CEO of the Center for Coaching Certification and the Center for Coaching Solutions. As the Guide from the Side®, she is among the best in training, consulting, conflict management, and coaching. Cathy has presented, trained, and facilitated thousands of events, workshops, certification courses, and organizational retreats.

Cathy has earned the following: MCC with the ICF, Certified Master Coach Trainer, Certified Master Coach, Certified Consumer Credit Counselor, Real Estate Broker, Certified Apartment Manager, Certified Family Mediator, Certified Civil Mediator, Certificate of Excellence in Nonprofit Leadership and Management, Certification in the Drucker Self-Assessment Tool, Grief Support Group Facilitator, Certified Trainer/Facilitator, and Certified DISC Practitioner.

Her three coaching niche areas include Business Development, Communication and Conflict, and Intentional Choices. Cathy balances training other coaches, coaching up to 12 individual clients at a time, writing and publishing, and volunteering.

Cathy's personal mission statement is "People". Focused on empowering others, Cathy is known for her passion to support others achieving the results they desire.

Cathy@CoachCert.com

Project Managers Coach

Ruth Pearce

Introduction

From the title of this chapter, you may think that I am advocating that project managers hire a coach. Of course, I believe most people benefit from having a coach and that includes project managers. My focus here though is on the idea that project managers *learn coaching skills*. Project managers who learn coaching skills – formally or informally – will get the best out of their teams and stakeholders.

Pushing or Pulling?

I love conferences and attend as many as time and budget will allow. I love all the new perspectives and opportunities to learn new things. Recently, I attended a conference for project managers. In one very interactive breakout session, I was sitting with six other project managers. The presenter told us to work as a team to answer a questionnaire. The first question in the questionnaire involved completing pairs of names in a list. For example, if the question said "Jack" we were to provide the answer "Jill." If it said, "Victoria," we were to answer, "Albert," although one Canadian said, "sponge" and someone else said, "plum." At any rate, you get the idea! The speaker's intent was for us to work together to work out the answers *together*. I love that kind of challenge and I love teams, so I was excited. Like several others I leaned over the table to look at the list. Just as we did so, one of the team said, "I can fill them all in if you like. I know them all." Some members of the group were excited as they were quite determined to beat the other tables, and somebody handed our colleague the sheet of paper.

What struck me was that we were far from being a team. No one asked any questions, no one solicited ideas from others, and the focus was on winning the competition even though there was no prize other than the experience of learning from the session! We certainly did not demonstrate collaboration at its best. As the team proceeded through the questionnaire, the process remained the same as one by one people jumped on the topics with which they were familiar.

This experience reminded me of many project experiences and it struck me in that moment that many project managers feel pressured to push teams in a direction; that it is their job to construct an entire plan; and maybe even that if they ask others for help it may be construed as not knowing how to do their job. In fact, I had a manager once who told me not to bother the team until I had my plan laid out. I was in a new organization working on a new product with an entirely new team!

Contrast that to another experience at the same event. My pair-and-share partner on this occasion was a project manager from an organization short on project managers and process. He believed strongly that it was essential for the organization to embrace project management to build success. He was already building a case for having more project managers in the organization. When we discussed his role, he told me that he, "teases out the ideas others don't even know that they have," and "draws out the best in people." Fascinated, I asked him how he does it and he answered, "I ask lots of questions!" He added that they often know what they want, they just don't know how to articulate it, and if they don't know what they want, the right questions get them there. Working with this partner was entirely different than working with the first group. Throughout our time together, he paid attention, listened closely, and asked questions.

These experiences really got me thinking about the power of coaching skills to empower project managers.

> *...the power of coaching skills to empower project managers.*

WHERE COACHING MEETS PROJECT MANAGEMENT

For thirty years I have been a project manager, managing everything from large, complex international projects to local conferences. As an accredited project manager, I have seen organizations and colleagues alike focus on three core competencies. Wherever I have worked, it appears we are all about designing the actions (tasks), planning and goal setting (creating the project plan and identifying the milestones), and then managing progress and accountability (holding status meetings, checking in with team members). Of course, these three competencies are not just the domain of the project manager, they are also three key elements of coaching.

It appears these three competencies are where the similarity between project managers and coaches ends! Where popular perceptions of coaches include cheerleader, someone who helps others reach their potential or achieve a goal, and accountability partner, or a sounding board, a popular view of project managers is the person with the clipboard, checking off tasks as they are completed. From my research (results are available on my website), project managers are variously described as essential to project success, micromanagers, the key point of contact, and sometimes the biggest obstacle to getting things done. It seems that while these three competencies are supposed to be our sweet spot, often they are not, or at least not from the perspective of those we project manage. Why is that?

I believe it is for three key reasons:
1. We don't have other competencies to complement and support our core organizing skills.

2. We often execute the three task and goal tracking-oriented competencies in isolation instead of collaborating with our project colleagues.

3. We are trained to *do* project management, focusing on tasks and action, the things that are visible to all including management and stakeholders. We are not trained to *be* project and people motivators, creating awareness of motivations, strengths, emotions, and thoughts about the goals ahead.

Learning coaching skills fills that gap.

WE ARE ALL PROJECT MANAGERS

The most prolonged and complicated project I have ever managed is my life. I am on duty every single day. It is full of change, uncertainty, resource shortages, and sometimes unwilling loved ones!

You are a project manager too. Whether or not that is your professional title or whether you have a credential, every day you are project managing your life. Life is a series of projects. If you have family, you may be project managing the lives of family members too. There is no business as usual, no standard operating procedure. Whether or not you are a good project manager in your life, your children or others around you are your apprentices, learning day by day and step by step how to manage their lives. I even think that for many credentialed project managers, this is the only apprenticeship they get. This may be a fourth reason that we are less effective. There are no classic project management superheroes – no exemplars to mimic. Indeed, another presenter at the same conference said that after more than 20 years as a project manager, he knows of zero exemplars, and his inspiration is movie characters. Just like everyone else, we learn from seeing our parents juggle the seemingly endless projects of daily life: bill paying, childcare, school, work, play, sports, music, dentist and doctors' appointments, meals, home maintenance, laundry, etc.

Seeing the challenge of engaging and motivating people, whether they be our family members, friends, or work colleagues, to take action and get things done, I am fascinated by the possibilities of integrating coaching skills with project management. It has taken a big part of my career to realize that the best project managers are coaches. Every project manager can benefit from coaching skills and coaching skills are straightforward to learn. It does mean seeking coach training. How much easier my early career might have been when enlisting team members to step up and get things done if I had coaching skills. How much easier it might have been if I had known to uncover team members' intrinsic motivation and align their goals with project goals.

> *... the best project managers are coaches.*

If coaching skills are useful to project managers and to the teams that they manage, what is the best way to learn them? It is often said that good project managers naturally coach the people around them. The best-known project management organization, the Project Management Institute (PMI), lists coaching as a necessary and desirable skill. So, maybe only people who can naturally coach are destined to be good project managers?

As a lifelong project manager, a trained coach, and as a coach trainer, I believe that every project manager will benefit from a coaching course. Why? Because even people with natural talent get better with guided training and practice, and those who may not have a natural talent for coaching can learn the skill. This is the essence of the growth mindset, that we can all learn to be better than we are from the start. The greats enhance their skills, others create new skills. It is a win-win.

WHO HAS THE TALENT?

Not yet convinced? Let's pause for a moment and consider the notion that good project managers have a natural talent for coaching. That is like saying that good project managers have a natural talent for organizational or communication or stakeholder management skills. Project manager certification programs approved by PMI specifically require project managers to take courses that teach organizational and communication skills.   Not so for coaching skills.

How often do coaching skills come naturally?   When confronted with a problem, are we more inclined to give suggestions or open-up the space for others to create a solution? Most tend to give solutions and learning coaching means learning to create the space for others to solve the challenge. Do we focus on how to move forward and what the next step should be, or on what has gone wrong and who made it happen? Research suggests that our natural filtering leads to conclusion forming.   It also suggests that negativity and confirmation biases mean that we are naturally backward looking rather than forward looking.

Are we more likely to look for and then use the answer someone else provides or act on our own solution?   Coaching is a process for people to find their own answers.   The power of coaching lies in the reality that we are most likely to work on our own solutions.

While some of us may have a talent for coaching, coaching is a skill.   It can be learned.   It can be developed.   It can be honed.

Coaching skills are useful in any walk of life and I believe they are especially helpful in project management.

YOU ARE YOUR OWN BEST EXPERT

When we coach, we trust our client to know what is best for them. They are their own best expert. If we stop coaching by falling into the trap of advising a client what to do, then at best we make them dependent on us and disempower them. At worst we leave them disconnected from their next steps and not buying into the plan we have prescribed.

The best plans are co-created with us playing a supporting role.

> *The best plans are co-created*
> *with us playing a supporting role.*

This is true for projects too, whether at home or at work. When project managers present the plan without consultation and collaboration, we receive stony faced looks. We may face whispers in the hallway such as "what do they know about getting these things done?" Or we may experience outright mutiny, with colleagues going off and doing their own thing, or worse, doing nothing. Plans created and imposed by the project manager rarely succeed because the only person behind the plan is the project manager. This is when project managers become whip-crackers and nags, micromanaging every action and task, and often feeling as though they are pushing the rock of Sisyphus up the hill.

The reality is that some days we must decide for the team and garner their support to make something happen. In those times when we as project manager must take the lead, trust and intimacy are critical, and direct communication built on prior active listening and powerful questioning come to the fore. Successful exertion of influence comes from prior groundwork and knowing the team.

Why would a project manager ever attempt to dictate the plan? There are many possible reasons including:

1. Direction from management.
2. The plan was developed before the project manager arrived.
3. A deadline was imposed and the plan seems to be the way to achieve it, regardless of feasibility.
4. The project manager is reluctant to ask the experts, believing that it's a sign of weakness or lack of ability.
5. A project manager new to a team has yet to develop the trust of team members or is perceived as unknowledgeable.

All these challenges can be overcome by a project manager with the appropriate competencies. Unfortunately, project managers are usually not specifically trained to engage the team in information gathering or planning. Project managers often lack skills for building trust and intimacy with their team members; they are not trained in clear, concise communication targeted at the learning styles of the various stakeholders. Project managers lack training in powerful questioning or active listening; they are not trained in learning styles, personality types, or other inter-relational skills.

> *Project managers lack training in powerful questioning or active listening...*

Even when it comes to action planning and accountability, the theoretical bread and butter of the project manager's role, the training tends to be technical and procedural. There is an emphasis on "what tools do I use?" "which tasks are due, completed, or behind?" Typical project management training does not focus on the inter-relational aspects.

THE STORY OF IDRIS

A few months ago, Idris, a project manager, asked me for some coaching. His team was spread across the world. He expressed some concern about the difficulties of time-zone differences.

During our first coaching session, we explored his goals for coaching. He laid out the following:
1. Create a plan to achieve the goals of the project.
2. Feel good in the role and connected with the team.
3. Feel relaxed at the end of the day.
4. Manage the amount of time on follow-up.

First, he decided to explore his goal to feel relaxed at the end of the day. When asked what that will look like and what will replace that sense of stress, he described relaxing over dinner and discussing the stories of the day, playing with his children before bed, having time to read something interesting, or watching a movie. He said in this new way of being he will leave work in his bag and be in the moment with his family.

He paused for a moment and reflected, "right now, I am checking email all the time in the evenings and over the weekend."

We explored what he wanted to happen for this vision of his evenings to become reality. What happened next felt like a journey through the basic competencies of coaching.

His first observation was that he spends time checking email because he does not trust that the team is doing what it is supposed to be doing. He checked his emails throughout the evening and weekends to see what was going on. He added that the project plan the team was working to was something he had put together based on a plan he had used on a previous project. He had taken little input from others on the team before delivering the project plan. Now, it felt to him that people were not really buying into the plan and were dragging their feet and putting obstacles in the way. He added that the team did not appear to trust the plan.

He said he was asking questions like, "Are you working on the task I assigned you?" or "Why are you doing that now?" or "Why did that happen/not happen?" The answers he received were one word or one sentence answers and he felt he did not have a clear understanding of where the project was, or whether things were getting done. When he asked, "will the task be completed on time?" his team members would invariably say, "yes" and then he would find out on the due date that the task was nowhere near complete.

In another example, he stated that he did not trust anyone else to take the minutes in project meetings. Consequently, he was not feeling totally present. He was not focusing on building relationships and trust. Instead, he was focusing on not getting blindsided by issues he was not aware of, or having the wool pulled over his eyes. He had seen leaders in his organization who were totally focused on whatever was happening at the time and he wanted to be like them. He wanted to have a presence and to feel confident that he would get what he needed from each interaction. He believed that if he had more presence, things would be easier for him and for the team.

THE POWER OF EFFECTIVE COMMUNICATION

In our second meeting, my client seemed a little glum. He reported that there had been a big meeting to discuss all the major projects underway and he had been asked to give a presentation to senior management. Not trusting his team to help him prepare for the meeting, he developed his presentation in isolation. He did not run through the presentation with others before the big meeting to ensure that he was able to get his points across effectively.

As he described how he prepared his presentation, he did not mention considering anything about his audience and seemed quite surprised several people asked for graphs and other visuals to clarify his message. Another attendee surprised him by asking him to draw something on a flipchart to illustrate his points. He shared that his slides were full of words with no visuals. Throughout the meeting he was also focused on the points he wanted to ensure he covered even if no one asked about them. "I was probably not really listening," he said.

During the presentation he promised to produce a paper outlining the key points of his presentation. He laughed as he revealed that his outline had been 13 pages long. "I wish I could have made my communication direct and to the point," he commented. Knowing that communication comprises up to 90% of the project managers role, he felt that he wanted to work on it.

He tied his communication challenges back to our previous discussion about monitoring his emails. Often the email chains became very long, and he would be emailing late at night trying to clarify something from earlier in the day. "Sometimes I may not be choosing the best mode of communication," he added. "Email is not always the way to go."

FINDING THE WAY FORWARD WITH COACHING

Idris started to explore options for tackling some of the challenges on the project. As he brainstormed, his list of options ranged from quitting his job to getting additional training. His eyes lit up at the idea of training. He commented that he has a great love of learning.

He mapped out his goals for his training:
1. Techniques to build trust.
2. Processes for co-creating project plans.
3. Understanding and planning communication.
4. Recognizing and respecting the way others process information.
5. Increasing his confidence in himself and his team.
6. Creating a presence.
7. Delegating or sharing tasks so that he can focus on conversations.
8. Asking questions that lead to elaboration and collaboration.
9. Building awareness.
10. Having fun!

We started to explore how he might find such a course. One option was to reach out to leaders he respected who had command and presence and ask them how they learned those skills. He also mentioned that he had twice been to a coach and both times he felt that he experienced the trust, presence, clear communication, and easy listening that he wanted to develop in himself for his team.

TRANSFORMATION THROUGH COACHING

A month passed before we met again. When he returned, he was enrolled in a coaching course. As we started the session I could see his excitement. I then asked Idris, "what has happened since we last met?" On this occasion, that was all it took for Idris to launch into a tale of transformation. In that month, he had accomplished a lot. He laid it out for me.

BUILDING TRUST BY SHOWING TRUST

He had found someone else who would take the minutes in meetings. He kept the responsibility for the final review of the minutes only, so he focused on running the meetings. He also asked the team about recording their meetings to listen again later. They agreed. He said he rarely used the recordings; it gave him a sense of confidence to know he had the option.

He told team members that he was limiting his emailing to workdays. He emphasized that he was accessible by phone. "If in doubt, call," was his advice to them. He said this helped him relax when he was at home, and his wife and children seemed to be happier. Occasionally he got a call; the time was manageable.

PRESENCE AND ACTIVE LISTENING

A bonus from delegating the minute-taking was that Idris was able to focus on what others were saying by listening closely. Consequently, he learned more and attendees felt comfortable sharing ideas. He said there seemed to be a newfound creativity on the team and they had come up with some ideas to speed up the project and hit some of the most important milestones sooner. This was building his confidence and that of the team.

POWERFUL QUESTIONS

The first thing he said he changed was his focus on what and how questions. He stopped asking, "are you working on....?" and instead asked, "what are you working on?" He said that single change totally altered the dynamics with his team members. Instead of giving him a shrug and a one-word answer, they told him about what was going on and why they were working on a certain task. Often, they explained that they were not working on the task assigned because they found a way to do things more quickly. Sometimes they had identified a previously unidentified dependency to add to the plan. Even asking a question as simple as, "how are things going?" resulted in him getting more information.

> *Even asking a question as simple as,*
> *"how are things going?"*
> *resulted in him getting more information.*

DIRECT COMMUNICATION

Idris said he felt he was able to speak clearly to the team and to stakeholders. He started experimenting with different forms of communication for the various stakeholder groups with whom he worked. He even tried out vlogging, recording his updates on five-minute videos to send by email. He found it had several benefits:

- Recordings created a personal connection.
- By combining a recording with a document, he satisfied different learning styles.
- He built presence because his team and sponsors were seeing him via the recordings.

Co-creating the Plan and Designing the Actions

He had called together all his team leads and had invited them to work with him to modify the project plan he had. He said he had invited them to throw out the entire project plan, if appropriate. He laughed as he described the way this group had started out saying the whole thing needed to be scrapped, and ultimately only changed about 20% of the plan. He noticed that they had a sense of ownership of the plan and were now just as much a part of keeping the team on track as he was.

Managing Progress and Accountability

Having described the co-creation of the plan, Idris went on to talk about the role of managing progress and accountability. He was excited to report that he was no longer the micromanager or team nag! It was still his responsibility to manage the project, report on progress, and coordinate problem solving when obstacles arose. Now it was a team effort. There were others helping to drive things forward. He felt well-informed about what was happening. He was managing progress instead of driving progress. By adopting coaching principles, Idris's success with project management improved.

His biggest sources of satisfaction were that the team was working effectively and there was a sense of trust within the team that made it easier to handle the inevitable bumps in the road. With a few small changes, project management had become fun again! He said he planned to continue working on positive changes and the few he had implemented had already made a big difference from his perspective. People wanted to work with and for him as a project manager.

OPPORTUNITIES FOR PROJECT MANAGERS

As I look back over my career and consider my most and least successful projects, I can see that the difference was in those core elements of trust, presence, listening, co-creation of the project plan, clear direct communication, and powerful questions. When I think of projects that got into trouble that we successfully turned around, the way out was through asking powerful questions, really listening to the answers, and building trust among the team to do what was required to get things back on track. The projects that ultimately failed? They all lacked these elements, the coaching competencies. What worked for Idris and has worked for me will work for all project managers. If every project manager is trained in coaching, the experience

If every project manager is trained in coaching, the experience of every project will be transformed for the project manager, the team, and the stakeholders.

of every project will be transformed for the project manager, the team, and the stakeholders. With a coaching mentality, project managers and their teams will have a higher chance of success and more fun along the way!

Maybe one day coaching skills will be part of the curriculum for project manager certification. In the meantime, my call to project managers is to learn to coach and practice being project and people motivators instead of doing project management!

Figure 1: Highlighting the core competencies of project managers who coach. Coaching PMs are the best PMs.

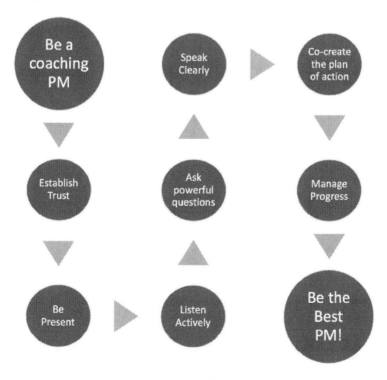

Ruth Pearce believes project managers are the lynchpin of organizational change and success. She has been a project manager of large-scale, international, complex projects for twenty-five years. Now she focuses on ways that you, as a project motivator, can achieve your greatest goals by building coaching skills and cultivating character strengths in your teams. Based on her extensive experience in team building and project management, Ruth calls upon all project managers to take the lead in creating a positive employee experience.

She is the founder of ALLE LLC which provides project motivation services as well as individual and group coaching for project managers who want to feel engaged and be engaging in their work. Ruth also coaches clients struggling with anxiety and phobias and is a licensed consultant of The Thrive Programme®. Ruth holds her PMP and PMP-ACP credentials from the Project Management Institute and is an ACC accredited with the International Coach Federation. She speaks about the role of Project Managers as team motivators at events locally and nationally.

Her book, "Be A Project Motivator: Unlock the Secrets of Strengths-Based Project Management" is published by Berrett-Koehler.

http://www.projectmotivator.com

Success and Magic of Executive Coaching
Wayne L. Anderson

How do Executives Perceive Success?

It is typically understood that success looks different to each of us. To some it is money, to some it is their health, and to others, professional achievement. What about executives? Do executives all have a different perception of success or is there a common definition to which they all aspire? If a common perception, is this the foundation upon which to build a successful coaching program for the individual executive?

> *...success looks different to each of us.*

To determine if there is a common way that executives perceive success, it starts with determining what they think about. It turns out there are several factors that executives think about that helps form their perception of success. These factors are both internal and external. (By internal, I mean inside their organizations versus external or outside their organizations.)

Executives think a lot about winning. They think about winning in both the internal and external environments. Regardless of which environment we are discussing, winning to an executive is usually short lived. Executives live in an extremely competitive world where there is always one more crisis to solve. More significantly, the crisis they solved yesterday is pretty much forgotten.

From an internal perspective, they think about things such as company growth, department growth, staffing requirements, and of course, financial growth. Externally, they think about the economy, labor force availability, technological changes, and legal issues. Some executives care about environmental issues as well as the political climate. (These environments are both dynamic and complex.) Their perceived success is largely determined by how well they manage the impact these diverse issues have on their company, their employees, and themselves. The executive develops a knowledge and understanding of these environments over many years. In addition, these environments are constantly changing. For example, the internal environment could be particularly challenging today since there are now four generations in the workforce with different work ethics, communication styles, and reward systems.

The perception of executive success is based on how effectively they utilize all these factors when doing two things: getting the job done and developing their people. Therefore, they focus on ensuring they develop the skills and competencies to do the things they think about and on which they are measured.

> *...success is ...getting the job done and developing their people.*

The painstaking events and situations that help the executive to manage in this complex world is invisible to us. Sometimes, they even appear to be performing magic.

DOES EXECUTIVE COACHING HAVE TO BE MAGICAL?

Have you ever wondered how executives do what they do? As previously mentioned, they operate in an extremely complex world. They seem to accomplish complicated tasks with ease. It looks magical. This means that the way they are coached ideally also appears to be magical.

What do you think about when you hear the word magic or magical? Do you think of illusions? Illusions that make you feel what they are doing is utterly impossible. Do you think of the paranormal? That is, people (or beings) with extraordinary powers that can control natural elements. Or do you simply think of a book or movie that uses supernatural elements to direct the story?

So, what is magic really? Many of us think about magic in terms of special powers, charms, or chants and spells that make things happened, good or bad, that is otherwise impossible.

When I observe the actions, performance, and results of many of the executives I coach, they truly appear to perform magic.

Achieving their results is as though they are using extraordinary powers that they have received from a supernatural source. What is also interesting is that the people in their organizations tend to feel the same way!

It is common to look at the tasks given to executives and strongly believe it is impossible for any mortal human being to accomplish. Executives accomplish the tasks and many times they exceed the mission parameters. They make it look so easy that to us mere mortals, it appears to be magic. They also can be observed doing it with a charisma that causes others to follow.

As an executive coach, I was forced to ask myself, what coaching magic will I perform to assist these individuals in being successful in their field of endeavor? I believe that to effectively answer that question meant studying both what successful executives do and how they do it. I examined how executives can make complex, extraordinary objectives and responsibilities look so easy to accomplish. I developed an understanding of the magic I want my coaching to provide.

My research and thought process took me back to when I was first asked if I wanted to learn to play golf. I remember thinking that playing golf cannot be that difficult. I had watched the Professional Golf Association (PGA) and Ladies Professional Golf Association (LPGA) tournaments on television. I watched adults hit a little ball as far as they could just to walk after it and do it again. I kept thinking it just cannot be that difficult. In addition, why would I pay someone for lessons to repeatedly perform that simple act? Of course, once I got on the course, I slammed it into the woods on the left (i.e. a hook shot). Then I smashed it to the right to some undermined location that was off the golf course.

I had trouble understanding what was happening. Why did I think this game was so easy? I remembered how the professional golfers made it look so easy on television. I was missing the things they did to get to that professional level. I forgot to consider the 14 or 15 hours a day they practiced. I was unaware of the hundreds of balls they hit just to perfect their swing or the hundreds of balls they hit just to place the ball exactly where they wanted it on the course. The many hours they spent each week learning to control the spin of the ball was invisible to me. That is when I had an epiphany.

Executives spend years going through many things that were invisible to the average person. They became extremely educated on the multitude of internal and external factors that were previously mentioned. We only see the result.

Therefore, to be effective at coaching an executive, I wanted to understand exactly what they went through to get to their level. I had to know the skills and competencies they develop to be successful. More importantly, I wanted to understand what coaching process to follow to be successful. The application of my in-depth knowledge in these areas was to make the coaching of these individuals look easy… almost magical.

Fortunately, I had a good perspective since I spent thirty-five years in the corporate world, mostly in senior management and executive positions. It was still important for me to understand the skills and competencies required in today's environment.

EXECUTIVE SKILLS AND COMPETENCIES

The coach must understand the areas for the executive to develop to be successful. This means that the coach learn two things: what skills and competencies are required and the status of the executive's development in those areas. The executive and coach can then co-create the coaching process that most effectively supports the executive.

…co-create the coaching process that most effectively supports…

The first important thing for a coach to understand is that executives are expected to develop leadership skills. This is very different from both managerial skills and technical skills. Technical skills are used by the person who is performing the work. Managerial skills are used when directly managing the technical worker or other managers. Managerial skills help to get the work done through the people over which the managers have direct control.

The executive must develop strong leadership skills and competencies. As a foundation, first understand the difference between skills and competencies. Skills are those things that an executive must learn to do their job effectively. They gain knowledge from learning and applying a variety of skills. Competency is an executive's characteristics that provide them with the ability to integrate their knowledge and skills in different ways. This empowers them to deliver exceptional performance in their complex environment.

In my company, the Leadership Science Institute, LSI, we have developed the following list of skills that our research determined an executive requires to be successful:

- Interpersonal Communications
- Problem Solving
- Conflict Management
- Developing a Vision
- Creating Goals and Objectives
- Time Management
- Leadership Success Principles
- Leadership Styles
- Multi-Location Organizations
- Basic Finance
- Multi-Generational Workforce

- Talent Planning
- People Development
- Negotiating
- Decision Making Techniques
- Systems Thinking
- Strategic Planning
- Presentation Skills
- Emotional Intelligence
- Crisis Management
- Change Management
- Innovative Thinking
- Coaching Skills

The following are the competencies we have determined an executive must have:

- Effective Delegation
- Techniques for Talent Development
- Ability to Motivate Top Performance
- Effective Communications
- Team Leadership
- Integrity
- Strategic Management
- Delivery of Vision, Mission, and Values
- Effective Decision-Making Process
- Development and Demonstration of Industry Knowledge
- Financial Management
- Influencing and Negotiating

Now that it is understood what is required of the executive to be a successful leader, the coach can assist the executive in their development in those areas. In addition, the coach helps the executive to develop the ability or competency to apply what they learned to the real world.

Let's examine what the coach does to accomplish these goals.

THE COACHING MAGIC

We have perceptions about the complex executive world. We have ideas about how an executive perceives success. We presuppose that executives must be effective leaders and that means developing the listed skills and abilities. Now we will look at how the coach partners with the executive effectively. In other words, what magic does the coach perform?

First and foremost, the coach considers the current skill and competency levels of the executive. The coach ideally has access to tools, such as assessments, that benchmark the status of the executive in key areas.

I prefer an Executive 360° Leadership Assessment. This type of assessment measures the executive in the listed competency areas. The executive is assessed with this tool by their boss, their peers, their direct reports, and themselves. The assessment will show how others see the executive in these areas versus where the executive sees themselves.

Next, explore the gap between where the executive currently is and where they want to be ideally. This results in gaining an understanding of the specific development requirements for this executive. For example, if the assessment shows that the executive is already strong in communicating vision, mission, and values, instead of working on that skill there can be a laser focus on development in a different area.

The coach will work with the executive to determine the skill development that is required based on the competency gaps depicted in the assessment. The skills can be grouped by competency and prioritized so that the most important development takes place first.

The coach partners with the executive to develop an Individual Development Plan, IDP, once the skills are grouped and prioritized. I suggest the coach and the executive work on the top three or four. This prevents overwhelming the executive. It will also significantly increase success. As you can imagine, executives are very busy people; if the list is too large, they will simply ignore it in favor of their other responsibilities.

The IDP contains the competencies being developed. It also contains the action steps to complete the development of each competency. The steps include any training and/or coaching to successfully accomplish the goal. In addition, include completion dates. At LSI, we include resources the executive will use to successfully achieve each step. Understanding this requirement up-front tends to make the execution of the IDP much smoother. Partner with the executive to establish the IDP.

The coach has things to do to prepare themselves for effectively working with the executive. Let's explore the important tasks.

> *The coach has things to do to prepare...*

First, and I think most importantly for the coach, is to learn the language of the executive. What I mean by that is executives use business lingo. Often there is a slight variation to the standard business language used by an executive and/or their organization. In addition, there may be specific terms used in the industry in which the executive is working. It is important to understand some of those key terms. Otherwise, it will be very difficult to communicate with the executive while supporting their development. By the way, I am not suggesting that you become an expert in the executive's business. Focus on learning the key terms used by that executive. Following are a couple of examples for learning the executive's language.

I was working with a bank executive. The expected outcome of one of his competency development areas was to see an increase in net accounts. Initially, I had no idea whether net accounts meant a type of client account, a line item on his profit and loss sheet, or some esoteric bank calculation. Regardless, what I did know was that it was an item on which he was being measured. I took time to learn that it was a calculation based on new accounts that were opened minus closed and/or cancelled accounts. It was one of the measurements used to determine if that bank branch was growing. During our coaching sessions, we constantly looked at the steps he was performing in his IDP for that competency and related them to the impact on his net accounts.

Another example was when I was coaching a Chief Financial Officer, CFO, for a construction materials company. They make the asphalt, cement, aggregate (i.e. rocks), etc. used to construct and build and/or repair roads and bridges. The expected result of a few of his competency items was to reduce his average sub-total variable cost, STVC, number. When he first told me that he was expected to reduce his STVC number, I wanted to know to what level his doctor wanted it. I am unsure how long it took him to stop laughing. When he finally composed himself, he told me that it was an acronym which meant sub-total variable cost. Essentially, it is the variable costs associated with his business; that was the term his industry used. Once he told me that, my college accounting jumped in my head and I immediately understood his language. For those who may not have a business background, it is the costs associated with producing a product that varies based on the amount of product being produced. For example, if he produced cement for two different clients, the cost of the materials, labor etc. is different for each client. His goal was to reduce the average variable costs. Just like the bank client, we looked at each of the development items in his IDP to determine the impact on his STVC. This was a number on which he was being measured. Reducing that number had an impact on his profits which in turn had an impact on his success. As a side note, the impact on his company and him personally once he completed his IDP was amazing… some may even say it was magical. His company significantly increased their profits. He was promoted to Chief Operating Officer, COO, of the company. At that time, we created a new IDP for him. Obviously, the competencies required to be a CFO were different than a COO. I am extremely happy to report that he was promoted to president of the company! THAT is the magic of coaching an executive using the right tools.

Enough about language. I think you get the importance of understanding the executive's language. Let's look at other areas where the coach must focus.

As coaches, hopefully we already understand personality styles. Whichever you are familiar with, i.e. Myers-Briggs, DISC, etc., is fine. I learned that they are all essentially based on the same initial research. The terminology may be slightly different;

each will place an individual in one of four areas or use four areas to describe an individual's personality. My business partner is working on her PhD in industrial organizational psychology. She used the same basic research to create our personality assessment called the L.E.A.D.180™. It takes the participant about ten minutes to complete and gets to the same answer as the others. We often administer it to clients as a part of our coaching process. Coaches are also hopefully familiar with personal interaction and communication techniques as well as learning styles.

An executive coach must understand leadership styles because once the coach understands leadership styles, they can use the insight in conjunction with the other areas to more effectively coach the executive. Let's first look at the leadership styles and then how the combination of styles can help frame the executive coaching sessions.

I know of nine different leadership styles. I will only cover a few here so that you get a sense of how to connect it.

- The **Autocratic** or **Authoritarian** leader – This leader makes the decisions by themselves. They are very controlling. As a result, they tend to closely supervise and control the people who are performing the tasks.
- The **Democratic** or **Participative** leader – This leader will include their people in the decision-making process.

They will generally reserve the right to make the final decision once the decision-making process is complete.

- The **Laissez-faire** or **Delegative** leader – This leader will allow the people to make their own decisions. Of course, as the leaders, they are still responsible for whatever decision is made. This leader will allow a greater amount of freedom and responsibility to get the work done. The obvious challenge for this type of leader is having competent people.

- The **Charismatic** leader – This leader focuses on creating energy and excitement towards the stated vision and mission. This leader usually inspires their people and is well liked, primarily because they emphasize appealing to the emotional side of the people.

- The **Servant** leader – This leader focuses on encouraging, supporting, and empowering people to operate at their full potential and abilities. This leader believes they work for their people and help them achieve their goals as well as the organization's goals.

There are two main things to remember. First, a leader may use a combination of these leadership styles. This is especially true if the executive has a large organization which contains different business units. The executive may use a different style for each business unit. The second, and possibly the most important thing to remember, is to know the executive's current leadership style and to which style they aspire. I believe you can see where this is important in the development of the IDP and determining which competencies are most important.

As a coach, you can begin to see how the other styles (i.e. personality styles, learning styles, communication styles, etc.) work in combination with the leadership style. For example, if the executive is choosing to be a democratic or participative type of leader, they must have strong communications skills. They must know how to listen well. They must have the type of personality that gives people leeway in determining their activities. In addition, they must possess a good balance across the various learning styles. On the flip side, they must understand the different styles of their people. This is something with which the coach can help the executive.

> *...the other styles (i.e. personality styles, learning styles, communication styles, etc.) work in combination with the leadership style.*

The next thing the coach focuses on is the executive's definition or perception of success and failure. This may be very different for each executive, even those in the same industry and/or company. For example, I spoke earlier about my bank client that focused on improving net accounts. That executive didn't care what type of accounts (i.e. business vs. individual). Success to them was all about the volume. Another executive in the same bank at a different branch also wanted to increase net accounts. Success to them was the number of business accounts specifically. This is important to the coach because of how they communicate with the executive. The coaching sessions stay on track when the coach understands how the executive perceives success and failure. The coach can help the executive to develop success principles and then relate those principles to the competencies defined in the IDP.

Finally, the coach must understand something about the executive's business environment or the organization's culture. For example, if the organization has a culture where it expects its executives to closely direct the activities of the people, helping the executive to develop a laissez-faire leadership style could be disastrous.

The important thing to know about the impact of this development process is that it affects more than the executive's work life. I had one executive tell me that his wife said she did not know what kind of magic Wayne was performing and that she still saw a difference in him... for the better!

> *...the impact of this development process is that it affects more than the executive's work life.*

At this point, there is one more important thing to do and that is to set up a process for monitoring and measuring the executive's development success.

MEASURING EXECUTIVE SUCCESS

The measurement of success is jointly developed by the executive and coach. The measurement process is based on the items in the IDP. Once developed, it is important to gain agreement of both the IDP and the measurement process with the executive's superior. By doing so, it ensures that there is support for the direction the executive's development is taking. In addition, it ensures the direction is consistent with how the superior perceives the executive's development. Most importantly, the superior then becomes a partner in the executive's development. I once experienced a situation where the executive thought there was an obstacle to completing one of their competency areas. During the IDP review with the superior, the superior said, "That's not an obstacle; I can handle that for you."

> *The measurement of success is jointly developed by the executive and coach.*

The coach is an accountability partner for the executive in terms of progress being made on the IDP items. You can do that by asking the executive how they want to be held accountable and checking in during coaching sessions. This will also help you and the executive determine if any adjustments are appropriate. For example, when I was reviewing the IDP with a sales executive, I learned they were recently promoted to COO of a newly acquired subsidiary. It forced the executive to change over half of the items in their IDP.

Of course, once all the items in the IDP are completed, reassessing the executive's skills and competencies validates successes and highlights new areas for development. This may also be done if the executive changes assignments.

SUMMARY

Executives perceive success differently. The coach seeks to understand what success and failure means to the executive. An assessment or assessments help benchmark where the executive currently stands as it relates to the skills and competencies to be successful. The coach assists the executive in the development of an IDP and then partners to hold the executive accountable for the implementation and success of the development process.

As an executive coach, realize and understand the impact of the executive's development on themselves, the organization, and the other people with whom they interact. The positive result of the work of the executive coach is pure magic.

Wayne L. Anderson is the senior Executive Leadership Coach, CEO, and Founder of the Leadership Science Institute, LLC. He is a Certified Master Coach. He is a senior executive with an equal blend of technical, business, managerial, and public-sector skills developed while working with Fortune 500 companies and local municipalities.

He has extensive experience in helping his clients to start, expand, and grow their businesses through coaching and training. In addition, he helps them to train and develop their professional staffs.

Wayne served as an Adjunct Professor in Business and Management at Front Range Community College, FRCC in Westminster, CO where he taught a variety of business courses. Today, he is a State appointed Business Advisor to the FRCC. As a Certified Business Advisor for the Small Business Administration's Small Business Development Centers, he helps businesses start, expand and grow.

Wayne is a U.S. Navy veteran with degrees in Organizational Leadership, Information Technology, and Business Finance. He is a keynote speaker on motivational topics.

www.leadershipscienceinstitute.com

EQUIPPING MANAGERS TO LEAD
Dr. Shelley Young Thompkins

THE BEST AND THE WORST

When employees stay under a bad leader for too long, it can be harmful for their careers and for their health. Studies have shown that when people experience this type of work environment, they are likely to become depressed, experience sleep disorders, stress, and exhaustion, both physical and mental.

Think about two leaders: one who brought out the best in you and then one who brought out the worst. Write down their names and under their names, list three adjectives that described how they made you feel.

Best: _____

_____ _____ _____

Worst: _____

_____ _____ _____

It is interesting when I do this exercise in a group and I ask which person came to mind first, most of the time, people think about the person that brought out the worst. I have heard it said that people may not remember the words you say, they do remember how you made them feel.

71

Now, write how productive and engaged you believe you were under each leader.

Best:

_____

Worst:

_____

If you are like most, the way the leader made you feel directly impacted your level of engagement and productivity. That is the reason it is so important for leaders to be equipped with the right skillset and mindset. Unfortunately, many are promoted to leadership roles without proper training.

MY OWN EXPERIENCES WITH LEADERSHIP

When I think about the reasons I left companies, it has been because of the poor relationship I had with my direct leader. I can even say that I have made lateral moves or taken a cut in pay and/or reduction in benefits, for the sake of working for someone that really brought out the best in me.

As I reflect upon the leader who stands out the most for me, the leader I consider to be my worst leader is the first that comes to mind. What is very present for me, even today, is how she made me feel. I was not alone in feeling mistreated as there were others that endured her wrath. While I will not take the time to unpack everything, suffice it to say that she made every attempt to discredit each employee while raising her own level of recognition. Who do you know that has experienced something similar?

This leader, like others, lacked basic soft skills including effective communication, empathy, and appropriate levels of discretion. Often, with this type of scenario, people are surprised by how someone was able to rise to the level of a leader. Perhaps they produced metrics that impressed the leadership team. What became clear to our team was that our leader lacked the people skills to manage a previously high performing team. This begs the question: what are the warning signs of poor leadership?

Unknowingly at first, this relationship put me on a very unhealthy path of daily stress, dissatisfaction, and eventually disengagement from the work I was so passionate about doing. I remember having heart palpitations, headaches, sleepless nights, and even the twitching of my eye on a regular basis. If you know about these symptoms, you know that if uncontrolled they lead down a deadly path to cardiovascular disease or mental illness. How many people are aware of these risks?

In this assignment, I was tasked with building an entire leadership development program with very limited resources, both financial as well as human. As a result, the assessment, program design, development of curriculum, and the delivery of content all had to be done by me alone. The fact that I did not have resources and that I was given such a tall order to fill was an exciting challenge for me. I consider myself a builder and this type of work and complexity is something I thoroughly enjoy and thrive on. Being able to both wear my strategic hat as well as roll up my sleeves to tackle the day-to-day details brought me great joy and a sense of accomplishment.

I found myself wrestling with extreme dichotomies daily. First was the reality that I loved the actual work I was doing and found it rewarding. On the other hand, I was unsure how long I could work in such a toxic environment. I became eager to complete the build out of this leadership development program as soon as possible so that I could move on with my life. Imagine the amount of productivity, satisfaction, and engagement I could have experienced if, while I was doing my best work, I was also supported and encouraged by my leader. I can only think about the amount of extra time and effort I would have put in to that assignment. What is the cost to individuals and organizations when poor leaders are in place?

To cope, I focused on completing my assignment in the allotted eight hours while limiting my interactions with my leader so that I could leave work as quickly as possible. I believe this scenario plays out every day in today's workforce. People are coming to work and putting in their time to get a paycheck and are unwilling to go the extra mile because of the toxicity of their work environment. All because of a bad leader. Is it really a bad leader or is the gap a lack of training or coaching for those who have been promoted to a leadership position? I believe it is a gap in preparing them for leadership.

LEADERSHIP DEVELOPMENT DOLLARS

What is the real reason for not properly preparing those who are promoted to the role of leader? Some might easily and mistakenly conclude that there is a lack of funding to commit to the development of leaders. Training organizations estimate that companies spend nearly $1.6 billion annually on training for employees.

Another study has shown that over $1 billion is spent annually on executive coaching alone. Many consulting firms boast about the effectiveness of this level of coaching and how it provides a return to the bottom line. I agree that there are benefits to executive coaching and it impacts on the bottom line. My recommendation is to divert some of the funds spent on executive coaching in the c-suite to be used on the development of frontline leaders. There will be an even greater return when you look at the level of direct influence frontline leaders have on employees.

Employee engagement has long been viewed as the greatest source for individual and organizational productivity. Studies have long shown that greater levels of productivity lead to higher levels of profitability. So how do we get great employee engagement? Let us start with understanding what causes an employee to be engaged.

Engaged employees are motivated by their frontline leaders. As a result, an engaged employee is more productive since they have positive feelings toward their employer. An engaged employee is empowered and believes they play a role in the success of their organization. They are absorbed by their work as they actively seek to positively influence the organization's reputation by doing their very best. In turn, engaged employees make the decision to invest discretionary effort and care about quality.

It is important to note that being engaged is a choice driven by the relationship with their leader that impacts employees cognitively, emotionally, and behaviorally. Having said that, one can see the importance of being closely connected to the employee.

> *...being engaged is a choice driven by the relationship with their leader...*

An executive leader tends to spend their time and effort on the strategic vision and guidance of an organization. As a result, they are less likely to make a difference in employee engagement.

Because it is the relationship that the employee has with their direct leader that feeds them cognitively, emotionally, and behaviorally, it is an effective frontline leader that causes them to feel satisfied and engaged.

Many organizations seek to measure employee engagement and satisfaction through annual surveys. One of the greatest benefits to measuring employee engagement is that it provides data that leaders can use to make improvements or focus on employee development. The insight from the data also allows targeted allocation of limited resources. Employee engagement surveys, while valuable, are focused on measuring the level of employee engagement. What is missing is insight to the reasons for the engagement level and the relationship employees have with their leader. While I believe in annual surveys, I also believe it is far more critical to evaluate results at the leader level and identify which leaders are effective. This will clearly show where focusing on the development of frontline leaders is important.

Organization often realize part of their success is based on employee satisfaction, so it makes sense to put development dollars and resources close to the people that will likely cause a shift in productivity and eventually the profitability of an organization. Chances are you have heard it said that people don't leave companies, they leave their leader. They are leaving their leaders. By investing in frontline leaders, organizations can change that outcome.

While it may seem an obvious solution to invest in the frontline leaders, as a coach it often means making the case to the organization or to the individual leader.

GROOMING FOR NEW LEADERS

For as long as I can remember, I have witnessed people being promoted to the role of leader because they excelled in their roles as individual contributors. I have seen this time and time again: the top sales person gets promoted or the best clinician is made nurse leader. The reason this is the natural progression is because, after all, they have excelled and so, in theory, they should be able to show others how to do likewise.

Many simply assume that the person is going to be able to succeed in their new role. I believe there is a fallacy in thinking that just because someone was able to exceed their sales quota or had the highest customer satisfaction rating they are going to be the best leaders. While the best workers may or may not make the best leaders, organizations continue to promote employees in this fashion. As an individual contributor they excelled; as a leader they may struggle. These great individual contributors can make great leaders with grooming.

Leading people is a whole lot different from leading projects or completing tasks. An interesting study showed that over 60%

of leaders were ranked fair to weak based on their ability to obtain employee commitment, build effective teams, and value their employees. New leaders who previously had focused on individual performance are now in a new role that requires a different focus. It also means different skills.

Our job as coaches is often to create awareness about grooming leaders with proper training and coaching. Proper training is more than instruction on how to complete performance review forms, make changes in the internal HR system, or approve timesheets or paid time-off requests. These tasks ultimately are far less important than making sure that the leader is equipped with the right skills so that all can succeed. Coaching is likewise more than helping them set goals and plan actions. More significantly, coaching creates awareness of leadership styles, perceptions, and the impact of how they interact.

Knowing how to empower and motivate team members requires both awareness of current perceptions and skills, plus an understanding of the people being managed. One key component of that is the ability to build a relationship with employees through effective communication, trust, and an authentic sense of caring.

Ideally individuals are groomed for the role of a leader before being promoted. When more organizations invest in this type of preparation and grooming, I believe the success rate of leaders, including higher rates of employee satisfaction and retention, will be higher. What does that look like? Preparing for the role of leader includes foundational steps that in some cases are overlooked. The foundational steps for preparing the prospective leader include:

1. Individual Assessments
2. Training
3. Mentoring
4. One-on-one Coaching

INDIVIDUAL ASSESSMENTS

Whether or not you use assessments and which assessments you use is determined by the benefit to an individual coaching client. There is research that shows giving an assessment without coaching can have a negative impact. For future leaders I recommend considering a personality assessment, an emotional intelligence assessment, and the 360-degree assessment. The order of using these assessments is also based on the individual. If they are not yet in a leadership role, you may decide to start with the personality and emotional intelligence assessments for self-awareness. If they are in a leadership role and unaware of how they are perceived, the 360 may be a good place to start.

> *Whether or not you use assessments and which assessments you use is determined by the benefit to an individual coaching client.*

The personality assessment is an objective tool that can help an individual better understand their internal wiring as well as their preferences for handling various situations and dealing with other people. When leaders understand themselves, and are also able to read other people, they can more readily and easily both relate with and guide those they lead. With this knowledge, leaders will be more effective at navigating the differences in their employees and at communicating, thus improving teamwork and increasing productivity.

There are a variety of personality assessments on the market. My personal favorite is the DISC; it is considered one of the leading personality assessment tools and is used by millions. DISC is easy to understand, easy to remember, and easy to complete with a minimal amount of time. Regardless of which personality style assessment is utilized, it will equip leaders so that they better understand themselves as well as others.

Another assessment that I believe provides an immeasurable amount of information to use in leader development is an emotional intelligence assessment. This is such a critical assessment because it leads to effective relationship management. Results have shown that when a leader has a low level of emotional intelligence they are more likely to dictate and impose their perspective on employees. A leader with a high level of emotional intelligence effectively supports and leads their teams consistently through change. The results of an emotional intelligence assessment can help identify how to work with a future leader for effective people management.

The 360-degree assessment gives insight on how a leader or future leader is perceived by others. In addition to showing areas of strength to build on, it will highlight areas for development. The information helps when coaching a leader so that they are aware of the importance behind building a culture of fairness, accountability, and trust.

Combine the personality assessment, the emotional intelligence assessment, and the 360-degree assessment for a complete picture of what an individual may want to work on.

> *Combine the personality assessment, the emotional intelligence assessment, and the 360-degree assessment for a complete picture of what an individual may want to work on.*

After completion of an assessment, the next step is for the individual to meet with a coach one-on-one to review the results and plan next steps. Assessments with coaching are invaluable in assisting leaders in their development. Studies on coaching show that 80% of those who received coaching built their confidence, improved work performance, enhanced their communication skills, and experienced improved relationships with others. The average return on investment for coaching is 600%. It is easy to imagine this being the case when you consider the negative impacts of poor leadership as compared with the outcomes of effective leadership. Assessments are one of many tools used in coaching.

TRAINING

Formal training in key leadership skills is essential. This can be done through workshops, seminars, classes, or conferences. The training can be a mixture of self-study as well as instructor-led training within a group setting. Selecting the topics often comes from the assessment tools.

Some foundational leadership topics to include are emotional intelligence, effective communication, decision making, giving and receiving feedback, facilitating meetings, critical thinking, delegation, change management, and growth mindset.

Coaching after training will increase the benefits of training because during coaching the leader talks about what they learned, how they are applying their learning, and co-creates a process for accountability to their follow-through. An additional benefit is that coaching is a skill set that serves leaders well. This means the coach is modeling many of the leadership skills so the emerging leader learns from the experience.

> *Coaching after training will increase the benefits of training...*

MENTORING

A mentor is someone with experience who passes on their wisdom and gives advice. The mentor can share insights on how the organization functions and observe the leader in action. Mentors are typically more senior employees and often in a job where they can create work opportunities so emerging leaders can practice their skills. Additionally, the emerging leader can shadow a mentor on the job. This gives the new leader a chance to observe the mentor manage people and provides the organization with a way to observe the style, behavior, and proficiency of this prospective leader.

When an individual works with a mentor, they have someone they can ask questions and someone to assist them with making business decisions.

ONE-ON-ONE COACHING

Having a coach gives emerging leaders a safe and confidential opportunity to create a development plan, explore possibilities, address potential risks, face setbacks with confidence, and move forward. With a coach the emerging leader will take what they gain from the assessments, training, and mentoring to the next level. By partnering with a coach, the leader will experience the benefits of someone who will hold them accountable.

A coach serves as a sounding board. A coach will partner with the future leader to expand and challenge their thinking. Through coaching, the future leader will consider different perspectives, develop strategies, and plan actions. A coach is an accountability partner and that includes being someone for the emerging leader to talk with about their challenges and their successes. I recommend the coaching relationship last a minimum of six months because meaningful change takes time.

EMOTIONAL INTELLIGENCE FOR FRONTLINE LEADERS

Why is managing emotions so important? Emotional intelligence is far more closely linked with success than IQ. A leader's level of emotional intelligence is a far greater predictor of their personal and team success than IQ. Being emotionally intelligent means that you recognize your own emotions as well as those of others, then manage them to work towards the development of successful relationships.

> *Emotional intelligence is far more closely linked with success than IQ.*

The relationships the leader has with his/her employees is a significant contributor to an employee's sense of empowerment and engagement. These employees in turn impact development and innovation for the organization. Successful leaders can connect emotionally with employees and adapt to their personal styles. The intentional act of seeing the world through the eyes of others to truly understand what makes them tick is a powerful skill for leaders. Developing emotional intelligence in frontline leaders can improve employee engagement, retention, and organizational success.

There is also a significant body of research suggesting that there is a correlation between emotional intelligence and satisfaction in life and on the job. This impacts job performance because it helps create a sense of belonging to an organization.

Being a successful leader means being able to influence change by sharing the vision with employees, engaging employees to be in alignment with that vision, and empowering them to do their part to execute on the vision. Additionally, the leader's attitude and behavior can significantly influence whether an employee remains with an organization.

Leaders seeking to generate results are well-served to be mindful of emotions in the workplace and how they flow within the organization. When a leader has a high level of emotional intelligence, they will retain employees, influence job satisfaction, deal well with uncertainty, and be more effective at making decisions. Successful leaders demonstrate effective communication and manage both social interactions and relationships productively.

While it may feel uncomfortable to some at first, a leader's effort to get to know their employees, show they care, seek to understand employees, and show employees that they are important pays great dividends. The positive relationship that can develop between employee and leader will improve employee engagement, empower productivity, and stimulate creativity.

So, let's go back to the beginning of the chapter when I asked about the best and worst leader you ever had, how they made you feel, and how they were able to impact your satisfaction and engagement on the job. Reflect on the implications of their development as leaders. In either case, you likely remember them because they were memorable for good reasons or for bad ones. In the end, it is those leaders who we consider great leaders that inspire us, encourage us, motivate us, and move us to do our best work.

Effective leaders can make a difference achieving both team and business goals. They are also instrumental in helping us to maintain a healthy state of being both in our work life and our personal life.

It is my hope that all leaders be trained properly before being put in a leadership role. Developed leaders make us feel like we can do anything, that we are important, and a contributor to the success of the organization. It is possible! Yes. All of this can be achieved when organizations commit to the development of their leaders. This type of commitment transforms organizations, providing them with a competitive advantage over other organizations in their industry.

Investing in the development of individuals prior to promoting them to the role of leader with assessments, training, a mentor, and a coach to meet their developmental areas ensures employee, leader, and organizational success. It helps retain talent. The employee can experience a high level of job satisfaction and engagement, thus increasing their likelihood to remain with the organization.

The leader will be in a much better position to lead their teams confidently, deal with interpersonal challenges, and face challenges. Studies have shown that there is a direct correlation between employee satisfaction and engagement with higher levels of productivity that leads to increased profitability. The organization ultimately benefits. The leader benefits. Each employee in the organization benefits.

 Dr. Shelley Thompkins is a Certified Master Coach and business consultant with her firm, Envision3. She specializes in helping people and organizations move beyond their challenges. Shelley has been recognized for her leadership in emotional intelligence, talent development, and organizational development. She has developed and delivered over 600 training programs and seminars. She also serves as a Senior Faculty member with the Center for Creative Leadership.

Shelley has over 20 years of experience in market-leading, Fortune 500 organizations such as TIAA, Wells Fargo, IBM, HP, UVA Health System, Coca-Cola, and Xerox. She holds a Bachelor of Arts from Howard University, a Master of Business Administration from American University, a Master of Theological Studies from Emory University, and a PhD in Business Management from Capella University.

She is the founder and President of the Charlotte Corporate Women's Network, providing professional development and networking opportunities. She also hosts an online cooking show, *Chef Shelley Thompkins*, on YouTube and has published a companion cookbook, *"Delicious, Simple and Healthier Recipes for People on the Go"*. Shelley is married to the love of her life, Kurtis. They have two adult daughters and a grandson.

www.envision3.com

COACHING ENTREPRENEURS FOR BRANDING
Lisa Foster

WHY COACH FOR BRANDING?

The brand is often the most valuable asset of a business. In the early stages of business building, many entrepreneurs are focused on the technical aspects of creating a business and miss the opportunity to define the unique and inspirational elements that will help their brand rise above the competition.

The coaching process and coaching questions are an effective tool so clients define what connects their brand to their audience and makes it stand out. Most coaching clients in start-up or early stage entrepreneurship have a fervent belief in their product and only a vague idea of how to express it effectively. Many of them turn to expensive branding firms who can help them clarify the essence of their brand.

Coaching offers a more authentic, less expensive, powerful, and effective way to elicit the same material for your client. The brand is their idea, and no one knows better than the inventor about the key appeal and intention. Coaching helps people become aware of their own possibilities. It is a perfect setting for helping people distill their vision into a succinct branding brief that can become the basis for other company identity collateral including a logo, website, business cards, letterhead, and marketing materials.

Branding is the human expression of a company, product, or service. If the company were a person, the brand is the face. It is the clearest expression of a product or company, the part that is constant even if a product or service is updated or a new one launched. There are five key elements that flesh out the personality and purpose:

1. Founding Story
2. Unique Emotional Proposition
3. Mission, Vision, and Positioning Statements
4. Competitive Review
5. Brand Personality

These connect the product or service to the target audience. In this chapter I will identify each brand element and discuss how to elicit the fullest creative expression of brand ideas from your client, and then hone them into powerful, key expressions.

> *Branding is the human expression of*
> *a company, product, or service.*

The process for finding expressions that define a brand are well known to marketing professionals. Let me illustrate with a brief recap of Malcom Gladwell's 1999 story for the New Yorker, "True Colors." In it, he tells the story of Ilon Spect, a young, creative female in 1973. She worked for the advertising firm with the L'Oreal account. They were having trouble marketing a home hair color that cost more than other brands, a product field that was very price sensitive. After a frustrating meeting, she became emotional, sat down by herself, and wrote a long rant. She let herself express her frustrations freely, writing as if she were the woman the product was designed for, going through the many reasons she was willing to pay more. The rant ended with the four words that famously defined the brand: Because I'm Worth It.™

These four words spoke to a generation of women who found in this phrase the embodiment of the self-worth they wanted to feel and own. The phrase became the definition of the entire L'Oreal brand and are still used in their advertising today. From one emotional experience, Spect generated a powerful phrase that launched a multi-million-dollar brand.

The process that Spect used to find the most powerful expression of this brand follows a pattern that is familiar to professional writers everywhere. As a communications coach, I recognize the brainstorming flow of ideas that becomes the raw creative material for branding. I see the successive honing of that message into its sharpest, clearest expression. Finally, what emerges is a short phrase that speaks to an audience and connects consumers to a brand. This is the process of branding, the distilling of a person's or team's creative flow into the essence of what speaks to many.

THE BRANDING PROCESS

The branding process is a method for coaches to elicit creative raw material from clients and then help distill that message into its most powerful form. This is a process to be followed for each of the five brand elements. It is a three-part process to broadly articulate the ideas that drive the passion for products and services, and then selectively find the phrases and ideas that connect to their target audience.

> *The branding process is a method for coaches to elicit creative raw material from clients and then help distill that message into its most powerful form.*

1. **Brainstorm:** Start by using open-ended questions as a basis for a writing exercise. You may want the client to write the answers or simply let the client speak. Take notes. Ask them to repeat something if you miss it. Sometimes in repeating their idea, they reformulate stronger phrases. Without censoring, stopping, or judging, get all the information on each element possible. Let them talk until they are complete. Be clear that all ideas are good. The point is to get concepts articulated. Some will become more important later and some will be left behind. That is ok. It is important for the client at this point to feel safe articulating their emotions. Encourage them to let emotions build and be heard as you gather the important raw material that later will be culled through and reviewed.

2. **Review**: After brainstorming for a brand element, review what you captured. Read or reflect back the ideas the client articulated so that they hear their own words. Ask them to choose the most powerful of the ideas, the ones that speak to them and the brand most. Bold or underline their key phrases and powerful messages. Let details that are very personal and less universal fall to the background. Find and focus on what is most important. Within the free flow of ideas, find the most powerful expressions that support a human or emotional connection. Encourage the client to reformulate, re-word, or clarify ideas to make them stronger.

3. **Distill**: Now, take the bold face or underlined elements from the review session and formalize key ideas into a proper paragraph. Rearrange elements to emphasize the key ideas and create transitions between other ideas to support the key message. Often, in hindsight, what is last goes first, so encourage them to change the order and highlight the strongest expression. Once the paragraph is written, identify the key pitch within the paragraph, and extract the shortest essence of the brand element that you want to convey. It may be one powerful phrase, or it may be a sentence or two long. The longer paragraph version and shorter pitch version are both important brand expressions. These will be in the branding brief created through the coaching process.

Use the three-step process above on each of the five elements to generate raw material and successively hone that material into the essence of the brand. After all the elements are complete, it is time to put a branding brief together.

A full branding brief is 10-12 pages that the company can use for guidance in self-definition and promotion, plus for internal and external communications generated to inspire others to engage with the product. Photos, logos, and brand collateral such as business cards or letter-head will help the brief appeal visually. Beyond in-house use, it can be used to guide website designers, architects, interior designers, and graphic designers to unify the vision and visual representation of the brand.

In addition to the full brief, it is useful to generate a short-form branding brief, a one-page summary with the briefest expressions for each element. In a side-bar, explore adding key statistics or information about the company such as the founding date, founding team, and early accomplishments. The one-page brief is the most compelling summary of the ideas and information that define the company. This is essential for most PR opportunities.

You can additionally create a 2-3 page longer-form with more detail. This form adds key details and phrases that emerged from the brainstorming and distilling sessions. Each statement or headline has a few sentences expanding on its core appeal.

In this longer form, keep the key facts about the company in a sidebar. This can be used for in-depth PR opportunities (interviews, trade shows, etc.) and be sent to major prospective customers to convey the passion and emotion behind the brand.

Further coaching may include how they will use the phrases to inspire investors, loan officers, employees, and consumers to connect and believe in the brand.

If the client is spending significant resources on a company or product launch, budget one hour for each of the five elements to brainstorm and review. After all brand areas have been completed, a coaching hour is devoted to compiling the briefs and another to reviewing the final document. Ensure the client feels that their most compelling phrases are included and that the document is clear. Encourage the client to continue thinking about each element after the session and to feel free to add information that comes to mind. A six to eight-week engagement with 1 or 1.5-hour segments each week will result in a highly polished document. Longer engagements can use the resulting brand brief to help the client develop the ability to inspire and lead others in a shared vision and endeavor.

> *Ensure the client feels that their most compelling phrases are included and that the document is clear.*

THE FIVE BASIC ELEMENTS OF BRANDING

The five basic elements that make up brand identity, 1. Founding Story, 2. Unique Emotional Proposition, 3. Mission, Vision, and Positioning Statements, 4. Competitive Review, and 5. Brand Personality are sequenced in such a way as to build from one to the next. Generally, clients know their story. What is missing is to practice telling the story for maximum emotional impact. Once they clarify their story, the Unique Emotional Proposition can be identified. From there, the client will be empowered to creatively define the emotional expression for the Mission, Vision, and Positioning Statements. Then, the client completes a Competitive Review to see how their offering carves out an emotional niche in the marketplace. Finally, the client will be ready for the most creative, most abstract, and most challenging element, the Brand Personality.

If a business plan has been fully fleshed out, the client may already have expressions for some of these elements. Branding these statements differs from creating statements for a business plan. A business plan focuses on financial and business modeling benefits. Branding focuses on emotional benefits and impacts. For example, if the client has a Unique Value Proposition in a business plan, that's a good place to start in branding the Unique Emotional Proposition. The brand expression goes farther into how this product or service serves the emotional interests of the target audience.

FOUNDING STORIES

A compelling founding story becomes a way for consumers to connect to the brand through narrative.   Every brand has a story. The story must personify the emotional and practical benefits that the brand offers.   An authentic and personal story is the quintessential pathway for human connection.   Generally, it is useful for brands to have a few versions of the story.   For example, create a longer version for use on a webpage, a shorter one for a formal pitch, and a very short one that is elevator pitch material used in casual conversation, interviews, brochures, or anywhere that a seven second pitch is best.

Clients usually have strong personal experiences that gave rise to the creation of their company.   Often these are powerful and also cluttered stories.   Like the garage where many entrepreneurs start, there is a lot of stuff to be sorted through. The coach's job here is to help them let go of the personal details that are meaningful only to them, and to emphasize the essential details and emotional moments that express a larger human desire and resonate with their audience.

Here are questions to elicit the brand story:
- Talk about when you first came up with this idea.
- What started you thinking about developing this idea?
- Describe the moment you first thought this product or service was important.

- What did you hear, see, or do that gave you this idea?
- What were your feelings at that moment?
- What are the phrases or moments that you believe speak to other people as well?
- What here do you think speaks to you personally that might miss the mark with a wider audience?
- What are the key emotions you want people to feel when they read your story or connect with your brand?
- If you sum up the essence of your story in one sentence, what is it?

UNIQUE EMOTIONAL PROPOSITION

Every brand offers something unique in the marketplace, something that differentiates it from other products and brands. In a business plan, products and ideas start with a Unique Value Proposition. In branding, the Unique Emotional Proposition focuses on the unique emotional gift of this product or service. It is crucially important for the brand to articulate how this product will make people feel different and better than similar products. The Unique Emotional Proposition articulates what makes a product different.

For this brand element, and for the next two, use research about their industry. Clients are often reluctant to do the research on competitors, and the research is very important. Awareness of what else is out there and how different what they offer is will impact branding. They may want to go full steam ahead even with strong competition or they may want to consider risks, benefits, and alternatives.

A coach who helps entrepreneurs understand their industry and how they fit can save them significant time and money. Even if this product or service is truly new, breakout, or revolutionary, there is an industry that they are disrupting so it is important to anticipate.

For a new brand to articulate an offer, be clear about how this new brand fills a gap. It can be challenging for clients to see what is different about their offering for several reasons. Some clients have simply failed to do research on their industry. Some clients have done the research, and to them the reason their own solution is better is obvious, so they are unaware that they have to say it. By the time they are starting up a company and branding, many entrepreneurs have thought so much about how their company is innovating that it seems normal. If the client has trouble with what makes them unique, suggest time outside of coaching sessions to research the industry they are entering so that they are better prepared to consider more detailed branding elements.

Invite the client to voice specific ways that the product is emotionally unique and new with questions:

- Describe your product. What does it do?
- Who will want this product?
- How will this product make your customers feel?
- What will your customer feel or say when they first encounter your product?
- What key trends in your industry does your product address?
- What problem does your product or service solve?
- How will your product help in the future?
- What future trends will compel your audience to want this product?
- What data do you have indicating the demand for your product?
- Consider emotional, social, financial, and ecological measures of success. How will you measure success for this product?
- Who else is addressing this problem?
- How does their solution make their customers feel?
- How is your solution different?
- What are the strengths and weaknesses of your competition?
- What are your strengths and weaknesses?
- How does your product address market gaps?
- How does your product address emotional gaps?
- How do you describe your ideal customer? Describe their age, gender, nationality or ethnicity, values, and lifestyle.

MISSION, VISION, AND POSITIONING STATEMENTS

Mission, Vision, and Positioning Statements articulate how a company defines itself. Separately they define the lifestyle, the aspiration, and the ideal effects of the brand. Together they are a full definition of what the brand hopes to achieve in the world and for the world.

The Mission Statement defines what the brand aims to achieve in daily activities. The Mission Statement inspires the lifestyle of the brand, and the purpose of the work. Living according to the Mission Statement aligns very closely to the client's definition of success.

The Vision Statement idealizes the values that the company aims to uphold in its operations, and the overarching philosophy or principle that envisions the lifestyle the company wants to see, encourage, or support. For branding, the Vision Statement includes words that evoke emotion even when unemotional. For example, key words like clean, pure, transparent, powerful, and honest help express the kind of world the product or service aims to achieve.

There are two positioning statements that companies aim to define. A Customer Positioning Statement, CPS, idealizes how the company will present itself to customers and what it does for them. This includes a description of the ideal customer. It

103

may simply be a statement of who the product is intended for, expressed in the most appealing terms.

An Employee Positioning Statement, EPS, expresses benefits to the employees, and there may be more than one in the case of a larger organization with different departments. The positioning for sales personnel is likely different than positioning for warehouse employees. In a tight labor market such as we are experiencing now, it is essential to articulate the benefits of the brand to employees. This helps to attract the best talent and appeal to the growing pool of millennials who expect benefits beyond the monetary. A greater purpose appeals to older workers too and is included in job postings.

Clients often underestimate the different ways brands define themselves in different situations. Just as a person might have a range of clothes in their closet, from formal and Sunday best to casual Friday, weekend, or workout wear, companies will present different aspects of themselves at different times to different audiences.

Use the questions below to generate the key statements.
- Mission statement:
  o What is the daily action of your company and every team member?
  o What motivates the company in its daily operations?
  o What emotional interest is served by the mission?

- Vision Statement:
  - Describe an ideal image of what the world or market looks like when you achieve your purpose.
  - Paint a picture in words of the world as it will be when your product achieves its purpose.
  - How will people, objects, colors, landscapes, or cityscapes be better with your product?
  - What will your product do in the world?
  - What will your product do for the world?
  - How will you define success for this brand?
- Customer Positioning Statement
  - How does this product or service address the interests of your ideal customer?
  - Who is your ideal customer?
  - What is the emotional appeal of this product or service to them?
  - Fill in the blanks: our brand offers _____ for people who _____.
  - How will the customer's life be enhanced or improved by this product or service?
  - What will inspire people to believe your brand is good for them?
- Employee Positioning statement:
  - In addition to monetary compensation, what will inspire your employees to do their best every day?

o In addition to monetary compensation, what values does your company embody that attract employees who will be successful in this endeavor?

o Looking at the culture you will create in this company, describe two or three key emotional traits that will define and build cohesion and community among all employees.

COMPETITIVE REVIEW

Branding includes finding benchmarks for the new company to measure success. Spending time discovering what other brands offer in this space is crucial to understanding unique advantages and niches, and measures to focus on for success.

The closer in similarity one brand in an industry is to another, the more important brand clarity. The smallest differences may be the biggest identifying factor that draws customers to this brand. Consider beer. Although beers are generally similar, anyone who watches football knows which beer comes from Rocky Mountain spring water, which one comes from the country of Clydesdale horses, and which one is for you. These identifying phrases and images are what differentiates one beer from another, an identity that expresses taste.

> *The closer in similarity one brand in an industry is to another, the more important brand clarity.*

Push your clients to make the most of even tiny differences. Finding their niche in terms of performance, price, lifestyle, geographic area, and other differences carves out a competitive space and will go a long way to helping them focus on what will make them more successful as they go forward. The following information works best as a spreadsheet for gathering data, and then in the distilling process, creating a paragraph that analyzes the conclusions drawn from the data.

- Using a spreadsheet, list five competitors and for each find the following information:
  - o Brand name
  - o List of products and services offered
  - o Key benefits identified by the brand
  - o Motto, tagline, or often used phrases
  - o How do they identify their target audience? Lifestyle, age, ethnicity, region, etc.?
  - o What are the geographical limits of the competitor?
  - o What are the physical or production limits?
- Fill out your brand's information for each question above.
- Compare your information with the competitors.

Ask: How can you make sure your customers know how you are different?

Finding their niche...will go a long way to helping them focus on what will make them more successful as they go forward.

BRAND PERSONALITY

Like people, companies have a personality. Describing personality traits will help you and your team create a cohesive and identifiable brand. Personality traits are how the brand presents itself to the world, and how it communicates itself to the public. Is your brand extraverted or introverted? Cautious or adventurous? Loyal or free spirited? Bubbly, comforting, or reliable? These and other traits describe the characteristics that remain constant. These traits define company style in approaching situations from corporate branding to marketing. Metaphors help develop the tone and personality of the brand through verbal and visual images. Visuals, whether graphic or descriptive language that paints a picture in words, express and convey the tone, sensibility, message, and personality of the company.

Empowering your client to describe the personality traits and identify metaphors will help embody the brand and make it real for others. Brand visuals are the public face and persona of the company.

Coaching clients to creatively envision their brand in visual metaphors has many benefits. These visualizations will help them develop key elements to interface with their customers. With these metaphors, any good graphic artist will be able to develop a logo, stationary, web design, brand colors, fonts, packaging, promotional materials like brochures, and other branding expressions that match the founders' inner vision of their brand.

Getting good visual elements requires openness of mind and creativity at a higher level than the previous elements. Being playful, being open to every idea from the silly to the sublime, and inviting laughter, humor, and safe exploration are key.

- Describe five key personality traits of the brand.
  - o Sum up this trait in one sentence.
  - o Metaphor: What person, place, or thing embodies this trait?
  - o Image: Find an image or two that conveys this trait specifically and visually.
- If your brand were a celebrity, who is it?
- If your brand were a color, what color is it?
- If your brand were a food or restaurant, what is it?

THE FINAL DRAFT

After going through each of these elements, generating a large quantity of creative ideas and honing them down, the client has enough material to distill into a clean document usable for promotion, developing business plans, building support teams, and connecting with their customers. Each coach will have a different approach. Some encourage the customer to write down their notes and partner in editing and writing the final document. Others work with the client throughout the writing and editing. Co-create the best process for the client.

After the client has a branding brief, it is a useful tool to submit to graphic artists for logo, business card, stationary, signage, packaging, brochures, and other branding collateral. It is also useful for marketing, PR, job fairs, conventions, expos, and other customer-facing situations. Clients also use the powerful phrases in their everyday actions to inspire their team and customers to believe in and adopt the product or service. Inspiring others is one of the core jobs of leadership so having powerful phrases to call up at a moment's notice is a valuable tool for a rising executive.

Coaching further can focus on role playing and imagining conversations in which these phrases will be used to close a sale, hire an employee, or develop a marketing campaign. The power of inspirational leadership ultimately resides in the leader's belief in themselves, and their confidence in the product or service they champion. Using coaching to develop a branding brief gives clients a competitive edge. When the phrases that define their value come directly from their own creative process, it gives them authenticity. This in turn benefits their ability to inspire customers to believe and increases chances that they will succeed in the endeavor they have created.

 Lisa Foster, Ph.D. and Certified Professional Coach, specializes in coaching leaders and emerging leaders to become better at managing, communicating, inspiring, and motivating others. Dedicated to getting results, Lisa helps her clients develop skills that matter for success right now. She uses evidence-based methods, like Korn Ferry Leadership Architect and EQi-2.0, to identify skill gaps and help clients develop action-plans to gain leadership competencies. Lisa believes that everyone can develop the skills to persuade, inspire, and lead.

Lisa has deep experience as an entrepreneur and communications specialist. For 15 years she taught persuasive writing at USC and Harvard-Westlake School in Los Angeles. She became an eco-entrepreneur in 2005 as the founder of 1 Bag at a Time. She sold over 30 million reusable bags, built and managed a global supply chain, and became an industry leader. She sold her business in 2017.

Lisa believes that everyone can develop skills to persuade, inspire, and lead.

Lisa@lisadfostercoach.com

THE CULTURALLY COMPETENT COACH
Wilhelmina Parker

MY JOURNEY TO SELF AS AN INSTRUMENT

I am committed to doing good work to honor being.

Good work you ask? Yes, and it is my life work to set my leadership north star towards that course.

I am a cisgender, black woman, a Human Resources Practitioner, a coach, a student of our global environment, and a person who is determinedly on her way to the pinnacle of Maslow's hierarchy towards self-actualization and spiritual enlightenment.

I take poetic license in defiantly adding to Descartes words to say, "I think therefore I am; I exist therefore I will add to the greater good via the power and totality of my real being."

> *I exist therefore I will add to the greater good*
> *via the power and totality of my real being.*

I was born and raised in Ghana, West Africa from birth until I turned 20. As an ebony-skinned young woman growing up in Africa, I learned about fairness, equality, integrity, and success as a reward for putting in the work. I believed with all my heart that race, gender, all the 'isms (racism, sexism, etc.) did not matter and that the color of your skin was unimportant. I believed that challenging work and industrious application get you to your rightful place in life. I moved to the United States when I was 20 and brought those ideals with me.

I arrived in Daytona Beach, Florida as a young, idealistic woman. For the first 3-4 years in college in Florida, I took offense at all who talked about inequities or 'isms, racial or otherwise. I firmly believed that if we were all to stop complaining and adopt a can-do attitude then we were empowered to be successful.

I had my first awakening of cognitive dissonance after being racially profiled as I walked through a Halloween superstore searching for bargains for my then one and two-year-old daughters. There were other avid shoppers, all intent on finding that perfect costume, just like me, with one difference: I was the only black woman. I guess this singular honor, being black, entitled me to the honor of my own personal unwanted shadow by way of the security officer who kept following me around until I turned around in the middle of aisle 7 to find him at my elbow. He glared into my eyes with a suspicious and accusatory look and said, "lady, buy something here or get out." Bewildered, I got out empty handed, shamed, and confused; the fabric of my tattered mantle of my belief system ripped beyond repair. I had made the move from dangerously ignorant to cautiously aware.

I am 48 now and I know the 'isms do exist. Today I am grateful and empowered to embrace who I am and speak the truth that I have been given. As a seasoned Human Resources practitioner and coach with an Organizational Development and training background, I embrace and am grateful for the opportunity to add to the greater good in my practice as a coach and lead by example.

I choose to courageously use my strengths and talents to intelligently challenge sacred cows so that I may powerfully empower self and others, embrace allies who speak shared truth, and participate as a part of a wakened humanity who may together discover pathways that empower us, our networks, our relationships, and our sphere of influence.

Sounds good, right? Wish it came easy and neat. It did not, and the experience was a blessing. This awakening and staying woke was as challenging, natural, unnatural, messy, mysterious, and magical as the birthing process.

I cried and laughed, raged a bit, cringed a bunch, and in that journey, I learned to see the totality of myself as an instrument.

When I started to work for corporate America, on through to the non-profit sector, and ultimately transitioning into public service, there were very few people who looked like me, talked like me, thought like me, felt like me, or even sounded like me.

I kept trying to fit in; I was unable to that happen. I kept looking for my role models. I even attempted to flatten and smooth out my accent, and to look, feel, and think more mainstream. I did what I could to not be me. According to my cognitive schema, I was unsuccessful fitting in and being comfortable because I had not worked hard enough and thus I could not trust my own thoughts and opinions anymore. Change or fail is what I thought.

By that time in my early 30s, my journey into motherhood was well underway. I had been blessed with two beautiful daughters who looked like me, depended on me, and looked to me as their role model. I experienced inner angst as I sorted through what of me to discard and what of me, if anything, to keep. Over time, I realized that the problem wasn't me; I realized it was systemic and even though I got it, I found myself torn and presented with a reality which seemed to represent an untenable choice: prepare my daughters to survive and thrive in the US by helping them understand that bigotry and racism exist and risk disenchanting them, or whitewash the truth and encourage them to fall in line with a Eurocentric culture and ideal they could never realistically meet. I had to think deeply about a future for my daughters as they grew up and went to work in a world where we still had an active Ku Klux Klan. The answer was easy; logical even.

> *I had to think deeply about a future for my daughters…*

Lying to myself was one thing; lying to my daughters and teaching them my flawed world truth was unethical, unfair, and inappropriate. The reasoned choice was clear: teaching my beautiful daughters the truth according to who we were/are and guiding them to navigate beautifully, gracefully, courageously, and powerfully through this world was the only right choice. From that choice, God raised my new-found whole being truth because by then it had become spiritual. Thus began the journey to be authentic and the choice to stay focused on behaviors in alignment with values of being a good mother, extended to being a better person, a better professional, a better global citizen.

As I moved into coaching, part of my journey included giving myself permission to invite myself to the coaching relationship, all of me. My point is, after and in addition to the formal academic training and experience, I won a hard-fought battle to see and embrace the value of lived experience in my skin as a value added to the work I am called to do. Today I can say I am a better coach for having connected the dots.

INTEGRITY MATTERS

About five years ago I started to believe and share my truth that I despised the field of Human Resources because I questioned the validity of equality as a standard. Imagine that.

At the time I managed College Recruiting and Leadership Development as a Project Manager in a successful Fortune 500 publicly traded company; I was based in the Organizational Development branch of the HR Department. I held the certification of Senior Professional in Human Resources, SHRM, and I was convinced that the professionally held norms implied buying into an impossible ideal, one that was based on an assumption of equality and not equity. It seemed as if my role and my goal meant working to stay as close as possible to the Eurocentric ideal and speaking truth to that party line.

After some soul searching, I let my precious certification as an SPHR lapse because I did not feel connected to the body of work and knowledge. Then began an equity and inclusion education journey culminating in my joining forces and graduating from a training cohort, Government Alliance on Race and Equity, focused on breaking barriers and looking at people, government, and systems from an equity standpoint as opposed to an equality standpoint.

Equality and equity are different. Equality looks at providing the same to all or treating everybody the same way. Equity recognizes that there are differences so to create the level playing field means providing resources to ensure parity. Equity means treating people based on who they are in a way that they perceive as respectful.

Equality and equity are different.

For example, if a school system knows that the child of a single parent who lives beneath the poverty line comes to school with no breakfast and by 3rd period is nodding off and cannot concentrate, it is inhumane of the school to ignore the plight of that student and to expect that student to compete with other students who have all the advantages of a healthier environment. Building equity in this instance may mean to integrate a food program for students who fall beneath the poverty line. The intention is to provide a level the playing field for every student.

A system of equality is one where the institution compares outcomes of all without considering barriers. Equality implies that everyone gets the same teacher, so all outcomes should be the same, and turns a blind eye to any barriers. Another present-day example I became very connected to was Racial Equity. Racial Equity applies both common sense and justice to a system that has long been out of balance.

The moment I broke ranks with trying to fit in to what I could never be, I found my coaching sweet spot. Thence began a life-long journey to develop my niche where the same experiences which once confused and challenged became the refining tool to craft and shape me into the coach I am today. I rejoice to use my full self as an instrument to serve others; honing them to be the best and well-cut diamond they choose to and can be authentically. In this journey, I pray for Cultural Humility.

In this work, my stance is that cultural humility is very simple: meet each person where they are at without locking them into a box based on my perceived knowledge and or expectation/perception of who they are based on a pre-conceived ideal. It involves accepting that person as an individual. Even more importantly, it requires a coach's stance of personal humility and the capacity to remain open to the cultural identity aspects most important to another person.

For example, I was working with a high level African American executive after a 360-degree assessment. She had reported that her superior officer had criticized her for over-dressing, impugned her mannerisms as overly formal, and had given her substantial negative feedback in a performance appraisal about seeming aloof and distant without context and concrete actionable items. Apparently, the dress style of her superior (a Caucasian woman) was casual and the formal style of my client made her superior deeply uncomfortable. In our coaching dialogues, my client validated her position, refusing to change her manner of dress. She shared that African Americans in leadership (especially women) had to work twice as hard to look right to be considered professional and effective, even in their style of dress.

After several coaching sessions working on building up her emotional intelligence, I was startled to see my coachee show up in tears. There had been a division reorganization and she and other key staff of color had received functional demotions. The client shared a new organizational chart with names aligned to racial and ethnic origin and pointed out that the re-organization impacted African American leadership negatively and seemed to reflect implicit bias towards staff of color. She said this issue had created such an alienating climate that the micro-aggressions she had experienced had bled over into an assumption of her incompetence based on an incapacity of her supervisor to understand cultural nuances which fell outside of her realm of privilege. So deeply felt was my client's sense of outrage that she wanted to file a lawsuit and appeal to the Equal Employment Opportunity Commission.

Rather than negate her truth, I empathized and validated the depth of her feelings. I held the space her to share her story and provide examples of the perceived double standard. Though outside the realm of my experience, my ability to hear and acknowledge the depth of her pain and the helplessness she felt helped my client emerge from an angry stuck place to a place of healing and problem solving. We acknowledged her perception of the elephant in the room and bonded in an authentic experience where she unpacked her experiences. I utilized Cultural Humility in appreciating her truth and used Humble Inquiry by asking tentative heart felt questions.

> *...my ability to hear and acknowledge ... helped my client emerge ... to a place of healing and problem solving.*

What shifted the conversation in the most profound way was when I said, "I may not get where you are coming from. I have not experienced this exact experience. I feel and receive the depth and hurt you articulate." I asked, "what are you prepared to do to survive and thrive, be empowered, and impact the greater good?" I affirmed her knowledge and power by declaring, "I do not have the answer; you do." What I did NOT do was attempt to project, minimize, or place her in a box about what I thought I knew. The turning point for her was profound and noticeable, and we embarked on a solutions-brokering dialogue with her as the expert which empowered and shifted this coachee out of the trauma dialogue.

DISPARITIES, IMPLICIT OR OTHERWISE, EXIST

I am a firm believer in the value of diversity in our workforce, our country, and our environment. I also affirm and believe in the inalienable right of humankind to strive for authenticity and integrity, whatever that may be each person. That is a difficult statement to make because it implies that the racist and the neo-Nazi have a right to be who they are in their lives, except when it comes to breaking the law or impinging on another's freedom and quality of life.

Where do I draw that line in my personal coaching practice? Do I do the ostrich with my head in the sand or I do I call out the elephant in the room? Staying neutral is safe and for many years, I was that person who did everything in my power to negate unattractive complex nuances of the impact of perceived cultural incompetence. In the process, I was actively negating concerns about bias, implicit or otherwise, in lieu of a compulsion to see and have a logical premise. That is not okay. After all, I know and learned my truth. With that truth comes a clear-headed understanding that disparities are real. Let us own it.

The sum-total of 25 years as a working professional woman with dark skin from African extraction has proven to me that lying to myself, and/or to others, can be at worst lethal or at the very least unethical. Parenting helped cement the foundation for an empowerment lens which forced me to revise and refine my values as follows: discrimination and bigotry do exist, and awareness and empowerment mitigate the damage leading beyond surviving to thriving. Sometimes bad things happen to good people. Life can be unfair, so make lemonade. Lots and lots of lemonade; sweet, sweet lemonade liberally sweetened with a non-fructose, non-cancer causing, non-habit-forming variant of something sweet. Laugh a lot along the way. If clichés and learned dialogue are the only way you can stay present with someone who is working through pain and trauma, so be it. As long as you come from the heart, you can acknowledge your own humility and your intention to stay in partnership with the other. Caring, compassionate silence is okay too.   As a coach, you are not an expert on your coachee's life, they are their own best expert.

How?   With specific reference to the coaching situation where the coachee had received a functional demotion, I was able to bring the coachee to a place of acceptance because she was heard and not made to feel crazy.   That simple conversation opened a sacred pathway to a healing place where my client left feeling empowered, heard, and strengthened by my approach. She subsequently found a subtle, strategic way to introduce a training module which addressed implicit bias and offered it as part of a strategic planning retreat.   Because her supervisor did not feel accused and the resentful energy had been removed in lieu of a teaching and healing energy, the subtlety of the intervention was effective.   In this case, the lemonade was ample and sufficient to ease thirst for a multitude of others.

> *...bring the coachee to a place of acceptance*
> *because she was heard...*

EMPATHY AS A HEALING AGENT AND RESPECTING YOURSELF

I will continue to remember the day I had a téte-á-téte with a racist.   I will be forever grateful to this person.   This person was honest and clearly shared with me that they were uncomfortable with an immigrant, myself, taking a job meant for white people.

As jarring as that statement and interaction felt, it was cathartic because it broke through my stubbornly held beliefs that I was deficient in my interactions with people even remotely holding affinity with this belief system. I chose not to pander in attempting to change that rhetoric at the risk of my own psychological safety. I had learned that biased people do exist. People may not agree when you speak your truth and in that scenario it is ok to accept that as their challenge and their trauma.

I was doing training on interviewing skills for displaced workers. Most of the participants were white collar workers who had fallen on tough times. After the training, a well-dressed white woman asked if she could have a word in private. She then proceeded to share with me that she had a similar academic background and training, and she traced her ancestry in the US for generations. She then took the liberty of sharing that my presence doing this work constituted a slap in the face for all her people stood for and my presence implied greed, taking a job away from a hard-working law-abiding American, and a betrayal of my culture. She then shared that the one decent thing I could do was to go back home, back to Ghana, and help there. She hoped that people like me got the message eventually.

Though taken aback, I was able to empathize with the place of pain this was coming from and shared a sentiment about my gratitude for being a citizen of a country which believed in free speech, thus empowering her to speak honestly in this way. I promised that I continued to be committed to supporting her job quest. I believe she expected me to affirm a negative mental model by my getting irate, engaging in name calling, and losing my cool. Perhaps that would have reinforced a negative stereotype and strengthened her racist mental models. I remained calm and grateful that I may have helped create a new instinct, the respect to see a professional instead of my immigration status. Did it help? Well, I kept it together. Sometimes that is all one can do. I am unaware of how it felt for her. It felt good for me and I believe it was healing knowing that I acted with integrity and emotional intelligence.

THE UNIQUE VALUE OF THE CULTURALLY COMPETENT COACH

Imagine going to a doctor to tell him about a headache which never goes away. Now imagine your doctor telling you it is all in your head, repeatedly. He says, "you are imagining it" when you ask for clarification. Now imagine the same scenario where the doctor listens, can appreciate your feelings and symptoms, and can brainstorms ways to help the pain go away. Which kind of client system do you prefer? I firmly believe that all coaches, if they hold the coaching code of ethics sacrosanct, want to be of the latter type.

To make it more complicated, sometimes it is only by being or experiencing can that doctor understand and hear the pain.

126

Note: I said sometimes; empathy is not racially nor other defined. In my experience it helps if the coach understands and affirms the differences which make us unique. Being affirmed and validated can lead to acceptance and growth for the client. If that is the case and I can do so even more effectively via experience, I value and am grateful to utilize the totality of me in doing this healing work.

It can be difficult to hear the lament of a perceived inequity and not want to negate it because it is abhorrent. That, my friends, is cultural blindness.

Cultural blindness is characterized by those who assert that race and culture make no difference in how services are provided and people seen. This results in the application of a dominant cultural approach to all, ignoring the strengths and uniqueness of ethnically and racially diverse people.

There is a gentle wisdom to saying meaningfully, "I hear you" without diminishing pain or negating hurt. The ability to sit with a coachee and be present with them is beautiful. The culturally competent coach supports and is present for coachees to lean into their discomfort of accepting an ugly reality and then begin the work to help them to move through and forward.

Acceptance is key to moving forward. Sometimes you as the coach hear the pain and then help the coachee craft a language which moves them to victory as opposed to victimhood. Receive the coachee's pain by hearing it, and let them leave it in your safe, caring, understanding hands. Then they can move forward to build that muscle of resilience and strength so crucially critical if the 'ism is truly the issue. An understanding, listening ear can help the person being heard become free from the accompanying anger that comes with such trauma. Be a savvy coach who understands the modality of trauma and how it may manifest in coaching work.

> *An understanding, listening ear can help*
> *the person being heard become free ...*

TIPS FOR BECOMING A CULTURALLY COMPETENT COACH

- Understand that trauma exists and recognize how it manifests.
- Be deliberate in developing competence in Emotional Intelligence.
- Practice authenticity, empathy, and healthy boundaries.
- Be aware of the risk for clients of being a yes person bogged down in endless emotional mud from self-pitying, go nowhere thinking where victimhood is the being and words like authenticity and empathy lead you down a slippery slope of becoming a support group. The ICF has a beautiful set of boundaries which hold the coach accountable to elevating the coaching relationship

as sacrosanct. Out of the wisdom of the ICF Standards, I have distilled my own:

- Be there to affirm, validate, and move the client to action steps and positive movement.

- Empathy building does not mean shared victimhood, and affinity is not a get out of coaching and building productive outcomes free card.

- While listening deeply to your client for their closure so they can heal and affirm, your role is not a therapist. Seek solutions even if the core of the issue is an 'ism wild card.

- This is all about your client. What do they see? What do they want? What are you there for? Can the whole of your identity help move them through stuck stages to positive action?

- Your work is client centered. Consider that your shared affinity from life experience does not mean that you tell, guide, or direct.

- All aspects of your identity are equally important in terms of skillfully navigating the coaching relationship. You must be able to keep all aspects of the relationship in balance.

- You are a coach, ideally governed by ICF, so stay focused on doing no harm even if you are tempted to make it all about yourself by talking about your victimization and experiences.

129

- You are a coach who can accept and recognize diversity and oppression as a truth. Empower your client with that knowledge and work with them to define empowering self-talk and then continue moving forward.
- Use data. If there is data which supports and validates your client's feelings, state it, normalize it, depersonalize it, and move quickly to solutions.
- Beware of projecting your damage, baggage, and hurt, and thus triggering your client into stagnation and self-pity.
- Just because you think you see an elephant does not mean that it is an elephant.

There is a well-known parable about a group of blind men who come upon an elephant for the first time. Because they are unable to see, they explore by touching it. As you can imagine, the elephant is large, and each man is touching a different part of the elephant. The impression the one feeling the trunk has is very different from the one near the belly, the ear, the tail, or a leg. Each man describes what they find and says what they believe this thing is, and each has a different description and assessment. Because there is such a great difference, they start to question one another, and eventually become angry about the perceived lies. They are behaving in a normal, human way. Each is projecting their limited experience and perceptions to the whole elephant regardless of accuracy. As a coach, it is important to be open to more information and more experiences than merely your single story. In my work as a coach, I commit to work to allow the totality of different experiences to resonate in every dialogue, every journey, every coaching conversation. That is the compass point I set as my life goal.

> *As a coach, it is important to be open to more information and more experiences than merely your single story.*

Wilhelmina Esi Sekyiwa Parker is an experienced, emotionally intelligent leader, who possesses the capacity to engage, motivate, and challenge for best results.

As a naturalized American citizen and immigrant from Ghana, West Africa, she brings an empathic approach to working with diverse populations and has extensive experience working in a variety of group settings and organizational cultures.

In addition to possessing a Master's in organizational psychology and a Graduate Certification in Organizational Conflict Management, she held a certification for three years as a Senior Professional in Human Resources. An Organizational Development practitioner with 25+ years professional and leadership experience in a variety of environs (global and U.S; government city and federal, non-profit and for-profit sector) she he is currently the Training Officer for the City of Berkeley leading city-wide organizational training and leadership development from a strategic and change management perspective. Wilhelmina is also the founder and owner of Sankofa Solutions Inc. Wilhelmina describes herself as a "vision led pragmatist grounded in Humble & Appreciative Inquiry from a culturally ethical perspective".

One of her crowning achievements is to be the mother of two incredible young women, Paige and Julia Bentum.

TRAUMA COACHING: A NEW PERSPECTIVE

Melissa Tyler Todd

In the past few decades, there has been an alarming discovery of the prevalence and devastating effects of trauma in our society. Trauma affects people of all types, and for many it still hurts decades later. For example, research on trauma tells us that incidents that occur in childhood can adversely impact the permanent development of the human brain and can be a contributing factor to various psychiatric problems. Because trauma is so intense the impact is profound. The thoughts, feelings, images, and reactions are remembered for a long time. Regardless of whether a victim, offender, or bystander of a traumatic event, people often feel guilt, shame, and of course pain. These feelings may be directed internally and that can result in deep sadness or depression, or even suicidal thoughts. For others it leads to stress, denial, or disassociation. Alternatively, the feelings may be directed externally resulting in negative behaviors such as obsessive-compulsive actions, addiction, erratic or hyperactive activity, or even aggression. In each of these scenarios, it is a misguided attempt to escape. The desire is to again achieve the state of emotional safety that was felt before the trauma occurred.

> *The desire is to again achieve the state of emotional safety...*

GET READY: UNDERSTAND TRAUMA

Because trauma and the response to it is individualized, it may be ignored or hidden. It is when it is acknowledged that it is possible to heal and move forward. There is no universal definition of trauma; what might be traumatic to one person might not be to another. It is important for professionals that are working with individuals who have experienced a traumatic event to recognize and accept the impact of trauma. Be prepared to respond appropriately instead of overreacting or underreacting. More on that ahead.

Living with trauma is a difficult task. It requires a person to have the ability to deal with a normal life while the brain is spinning with emotions. Trauma can be a shattering experience. It tends to affect a person's identity in three specific ways:

1. Trauma can shatter a person's view of their competence and worth. Prior to the traumatic event, ideally people approach life with confidence. People tend to have a confident expectation that they can manage most situations that occur in their lives. Traumatic events challenge this expectation. These types of events can toss a person in to a circle of self-rejection, self-hatred, and worthlessness.

2. Traumatic events can destroy the basic assumption that the world is a safe and orderly place. Prior to the

traumatic event, most people are aware that bad things happen. At the same time, they operate with the illusion that bad things do not happen to them. This illusion is shattered after the traumatic event. These types of events make the person painfully aware that being careful and good does not protect them from bad things happening. Thus, they have difficulty holding onto the basic assumption that the world is safe and orderly. This can leave them living in a state of hyperawareness and uncertainty.

3. The emotional pain of the traumatic event can drive a person to withdraw from their family and community. Because trauma tends to cause a person to disconnect, most trauma survivors report a new strangeness about themselves. The traumatic event can leave a person feeling different from other people. The trauma even leaves them feeling cut off from the rest of the world. They are left feeling broken and damaged.

Avoiding the emotional pain of a traumatic event is a normal response and, there is a cost.

Traumatized people often develop three defense mechanisms to cope. These are known as repression, denial, and dissociation. Hopefully, they have addressed these defense mechanisms in counseling prior to entering coaching. If they have not, it will be imperative that the trauma coach be able to recognize if they are presenting with any of them so that they can be addressed.

1. Repression is a defense mechanism that is used to bury the painful experience. Repression is best known as the exclusion of distressing memories, thoughts, or feelings from the conscious mind. It is common for trauma survivors to present as guarded, showing little or no emotions. Repression can also block a person's ability to remember all or parts of the traumatic event.

2. Denial is the defense mechanism that involves perceptual distortion. Instead of the person seeing the traumatic event as it occurred, they tend to put a spin on the painful memories. They do this by editing, revising, and disinfecting them. Denial is often the default mode of the emotional side of the brain.

3. Dissociation is the last defense mechanism associated with trauma. It is a means of emotional and mental escape when the physical escape is impossible. This can be dangerous for the person surviving the trauma because it involves detachment from reality and can create an opportunity for psychosis. If a client presents with this, it is best to refer them to a trained mental health professional.

More people than we realize have experienced some sort of trauma. Remember, everyone responds to trauma differently and the impact of trauma varies. Trauma can impact individuals socially, psychologically, academically, neuro-physiologically, and socioeconomically. Trauma can also impair physical health. Because the feeling of being abandoned or endangered can cut very deep, it is essential to create awareness that it is possible to regain emotional safety. A new normal can be an opportunity to have something more than before by being open to the possibilities. It is scary to lose control and feel emotionally unsafe; it can also be liberating.

The increase of trauma and its effects on people has brought attention to the fact that better assistance in dealing with the trauma earlier and more effectively is in demand. There is also a call for better informed practices to assist people affected by trauma to reconnect with the world and themselves, plus reestablish their lives.

Thankfully, current research has shown that effects of the traumas can be worked through. It has been noted in several research studies that the trauma can be a precursor to the opportunity for people to experience increased confidence, deeper levels of love and intimacy, and a strong sense of purpose and meaning. It is now known that traumatic experiences only define a person or their future if it is allowed; instead trauma can create an opportunity to thrive.

> *...trauma can be a precursor to the opportunity for people to experience increased confidence, deeper levels of love and intimacy, and a strong sense of purpose and meaning.*

POST-TRAUMATIC GROWTH

In the mid-1990s, Richard G. Tedeschi and Lawrence G. Calhoun, two well-known psychologists at University of North Carolina, coined the term post-traumatic growth. Post-traumatic growth refers to the positive mental and emotional growth that can occur after a trauma. This growth is noticed in the ability to rise to a higher level of functioning. It was their research that gave life to the idea that instead of trauma paralyzing a person, it can be a learning and strengthening experience. They asserted that people with strong support systems, adaptability, and ability to learn coping skills are more likely to move past being victims and experience balance.

People that achieve post-traumatic grown have faced a momentous challenge. In doing so, they were able to gain a greater awareness of the world and understanding of their place in it. Most importantly, post-traumatic growth is about creating a new way of life and finding a new normal. At the same time, developing the adaptive coping skills and locating supportive resources can be challenging for people during traumatic suffering. Often, after trauma, people find themselves in dysfunctional family and social systems that are ill-equipped to assist them. The good news is that Tedeschi and Calhoun found that 90 percent of trauma survivors who did receive assistance report they then experienced some level of post-traumatic growth.

139

It is important that the trauma survivor has processed the trauma related to the memories and feelings that kept them in the trauma loop and discharged pent-up fight-or-flight energy. It is equally important to develop the ability and desire to recognize and manage feelings, and to be open to others. It means relearning to trust people and circumstances.

In the mid 1980's, Thomas Leonard, a financial planner, realized that his clients sought more than the standard financial advice. They wanted support to set and achieve goals, create strategies and action plans, and effectively manage their own lives. Because they were having difficulty, they were experiencing issues with situational depression and anxiety. It was at this time that he moved into a new profession that is now known as coaching. Through a properly delivered and understood process, coaching takes the client from where they are to where they want to be. It is the role of a trauma coach to help people minimize the time in traumatic suffering and offer them the opportunity to experience post-traumatic growth. There is a difference between surviving and thriving. Trauma coaches have a process and learned competencies to empower people to live and thrive after the traumatic event.

The focus of trauma coaching is not recovery. Recovery is about returning to the way of life that was before something happened. This is unachievable for a trauma survivor. Life after a trauma event will forever be different from the days prior to the trauma. Different can be an opportunity to create a desired state of being and life. Therefore, the focus of trauma coaching is relearning, redefining, and creating.

Relearning is a process of acquiring new knowledge and skills to adapt successfully to the new life. It has been defined as learning something again. For trauma survivors, it refers to relearning things that were stolen in the aftermath of the traumatic event.

Trauma coaching can help the trauma survivor reclaim their sense of competency and help them believe that the world is a safe and orderly place. Most of all, trauma coaching can empower trauma survivors to learn new skills that empower them to re-establish relationships with their family and reconnect to their community.

There are numerous specialties in the field of coaching. Trauma coaching is a relatively new field. Trauma coaches work with people that experienced traumatic events. Many people have become confused about the differences between coaching and counseling. Some individuals that have experienced a traumatic event might be best served by counseling to process the event before they are ready for trauma coaching. Some people are not responsive to traditional counseling. They are resistant to dealing with past issues and want to focus on the here and now, so they are well-served by trauma coaching. Trauma coaching is focused on altering existing conditions to meet future goals. While the past may be covered in coaching sessions, the past is discussed briefly with the purpose of shifting the way an individual understands the past or learning from the past for their present or new reality.

It seems the struggle a trauma survivor goes through to figure out and adapt to their life after trauma is a defining factor in creating the opportunity for growth after the trauma. Post-traumatic growth is the positive outcome due to successful utilization of skills and resources that follows a traumatic event. This often includes resilience, which is the innate emotional and psychological characteristics that support the potential for this positive outcome.

> *Post-traumatic growth is the positive outcome due to successful utilization of skills and resources that follows a traumatic event.*

Before the coaching can begin, it must be determined whether the trauma survivor will be best served by counseling, a combination of counseling and coaching, or coaching. A person still in crisis might postpone coaching until they are emotionally and physically prepared. After the determination is made that coaching is appropriate, there are steps that are effective for empowering a trauma survivor to move forward with the objective of experiencing post-traumatic growth.

TRAUMA COACHING

When working with individuals that have experienced a traumatic event, it is imperative to establish a safe and supportive environment. Often, the professionals are so interested in stopping the suffering that they immediately jump into reprocessing and assume that reprocessing is right for everyone. If you take away their coping skills of repression, denial, and dissociation, however maladaptive they may be, you are leaving them with nothing to use when their emotions run high. First, they must learn more productive skills.

> *...establish a safe and supportive environment.*

Trauma coaching concentrates on thoughts and behaviors. It works toward specific, measurable solutions to identified maladaptive behaviors. In this process, the emotions of the individual are regarded as cues that are used to examine thoughts and behavior, rather than being something to examine for their own purpose. Normally, this will also help with removing the emotional attachments that the individual has formed to the trauma. As a point of awareness, the attachment to a trauma provides a false sense of safety and stability because it feels less threatening to stay attached to what is familiar regardless of how harmful it is emotionally or physically. When empowered to choose and implement solutions, the trauma survivor begins the move to thriving.

Trauma coaching is useful to invite the trauma survivor to reclaim aspects of them self before the traumatic event occurred. Asking them to remember the last time they felt safety, joy, and peace can empower them to return to that state of being and feel connected to themselves and their surroundings.

In trauma coaching it is essential to identify methods to promote resiliency and find ways to ascertain resources for healthy living. As early as the 1960's researchers began looking at how resiliency factors play a role in the determination between long term negative psychological issues due to a traumatic event and moving forward effectively. In past years, resiliency was viewed as a trait. With their research, Tedeschi and Calhoun questioned this idea. In current studies, it has been shown that instead of being an individual characteristic, resilience is a process that is implemented by the individual. Thus, the research tells us that resiliency can be promoted and learned.

Researchers have identified that there are several elements that contribute to the psychological well-being of people. These elements include contextual factors such as the individual, family, and environment. It has been found that individuals that are facing adversity are more resilient when they are offered care and have relationships that create feelings of love and trust. These elements tend to provide encouragement and stability. Along with having healthy support systems, it has been found that individuals who have realistic thinking patterns, self-confidence, positive self-image, communications skills, and emotional control tend to be more resilient. A trauma coach can assist an individual to develop these things.

TRAUMA LOOP

Some people have experienced prolonged traumatic events. They tend to carry around the memory of these events in their everyday life. Similar events occur and thus they live in a state of traumatic suffering. The memories of these events can shape a person's identity, how they feel about themselves, and direct their behavior. This is known as living in a trauma loop.

The first step of trauma coaching in this scenario is to dissolve the trauma loop and the attachment to the story of the event. It is imperative to get people to stop telling the story of the event that caused the trauma because every time the person tells the story they experience the trauma again. It is common for a trauma survivor to feel attached to the story. Getting them to release the desire to tell the story can be challenging. Creating a new normal can be difficult or even terrifying. It is strange to believe that there is comfort in staying trapped in the trauma loop. Bouncing forward out of the loop requires faith and trust in the universe, self, and others. After a traumatic event, this can feel almost impossible. The fear of the unknown can be more powerful than the motivation to develop a new normal.

As it was pointed out to me many years ago, traumatic events in life tend to connect with each other. There tends to be a theme that runs from the beginning to the end just like a plot in a movie. Unfortunately, the movie continues endlessly. It keeps looping back around to a new trauma. Consider the reality a trauma victim in the loop is experiencing and partner with them where they are to move forward. Explore the motivations to stay in the trauma loop and then explore the motivations to dissolve it. Ask about readiness, desire, and small steps. Recognize the small wins and build on them to increase confidence. Explore the short-term, mid-term, and long-term outcomes.

COACHING FROM TRAUMA SURVIVOR TO THRIVING

Coaching is a practice with the basic premise that the client is their own best expert. This premise is especially useful in trauma coaching. Most trauma survivors have experiences that many other people cannot even imagine. It is important for a trauma coach to be mindful and respectful of this reality.

A trauma survivor seeking coaching is best served by their coach creating a safe space to explore future possibilities, define their own goals, and decide their own plan of action. By doing so, the trauma survivor is taking their first step back into the world and to feeling empowered by their own choices. Learning new coping skills, owning their own decisions, and creating their own new normal will give the client the confidence to take responsibility for the outcome.

Trauma coaching is an opportunity for considering and managing the impact of trauma on the physical, mental, emotional, behavioral, and spiritual aspects of human functioning. Because trauma coaching is goal-oriented, instead of focusing on assessment, diagnosis, and a treatment period, a trauma coach works in a partnership with trauma survivors to develop strategies for learning the adaptive coping skills and designing action steps to move toward their own goals. The premise of trauma coaching is that the client is the expert. This is very empowering for people that have experienced traumatic suffering. It empowers them to regain a sense of control of themselves, their surroundings, and their future.

TIPS FOR COACHING TRAUMA CLIENTS

Tip 1: Establish Trust and Build Rapport. It is common for individuals with traumatic events in their past to have mistrust and abuse issues. When working with them, it will be important that they feel safe in the relationship.

Tip 2: Stop the Repeat. Work with the client to end the repeat of the story by replacing it with an open space for growth. By ending the repeat, the client moves on.

Tip 3: Education is an Opportunity for the Client. Explore access to information regarding trauma, information on how trauma affects the body, and especially how trauma affects the brain. This will help clients understand the importance of better sleep habits, a good nutrition plan, and proper use of medications.

Tip 4: Build Feeling Vocabulary. Help clients build their vocabulary so they can better express feelings and better understand where they are emotionally. This will help assist with their emotional growth and create the opportunity to be emotionally mature.

Tip 5: Invite Sharing. Develop a method to assist the client with sharing their story regarding their trauma so they can begin to write a new ending. Hearing the new ending to the story out loud makes the potential become real. Being able to share it with a trusted individual also helps the client feel supported and prepared to open-up for future growth.

SELF-CARE TIPS FOR TRAUMA COACHES

Tip 1: Readiness Check-in. Before beginning to work with a person that is requesting trauma coaching, the coach starts by evaluating how they feel about trauma. If the coach is unprepared emotionally to work with the client, the client will

148

feel uncomfortable. It can create a barrier in the relationship and the coaching process will be affected. As a coach, explore your feelings on various traumas and your ability to openly discuss trauma. Reflect on your willingness to probe and to be comfortable being uncomfortable.

> *Reflect on your willingness to probe and*
> *to be comfortable being uncomfortable.*

Tip 2: Shed the Day. After working with trauma clients, it is important to have a way to shed the day. Using mindfulness is a good technique. It helps you feel grounded and focused on the here and now. A short mindful practice is:

1. Find a place that is both comfortable and quiet.
2. Close your eyes and focus on the dark space.
3. Slowly breathe in and out 4 times
4. Relax and repeat the exercise for 15 minutes.

Tip 3: Identify and Manage Compassion Fatigue. Compassion fatigue is different than burnout. Compassion Fatigue is more of a risk than burn-out. It can happen after working with only one client or can occur after a series of clients. Working with people that have experienced trauma can be very taxing on a coach. There can be emotional residue from the exposure of working with those that are dealing with the outcome of traumatic events. Managing fatigue requires a healthy balance between work and home. It is important to evaluate oneself on a regular basis to ensure that the coach can separate from the trauma challenges of the client.

Tip 4: Practice Self-care. It is common for individuals that work in high stress fields to experience burnout. This known as a state of physical, emotional, and mental exhaustion. It is imperative that a coach working with clients who have trauma issues also take care of themselves. It is important to have a regular routine that supports healthy eating and sleep patterns. Self-care also ideally includes an exercise program. It is imperative that trauma coaches have a wellness program of their own established.

SUMMARY

Trauma coaching is a specialized field of coaching. In addition to a trauma coach learning the competencies and skills of a professional coach and earning membership in the International Coach Federation, training in the field of trauma often makes sense. Credentialed coaches must demonstrate the ability to focus on the client showing individual attention and respect for them and their current position, ask powerful coaching questions, actively listen, develop trust and intimacy, and co-create the coaching relationship. In addition to these skills, a trauma coach requires patience. It is imperative that a trauma coach empowers the trauma survivor to determine the pace of their process. A trauma coach must have the skills to recognize maladaptive tendencies and handle unusual reactions without taking the trauma symptoms personally. A trauma coach addresses the trauma survivor's reality respectfully. Trauma coaching is a powerful way to support trauma survivors creating their new reality.

> *It is imperative that a trauma coach*
> *empowers the trauma survivor*
> *to determine the pace of their process.*

Melissa Tyler Todd holds several degrees in the field of human services and mental health counseling. She was a licensed professional counselor for over 25 years. Recently, she decided to leave the counseling profession and enter the world of professional coaching. Her specialty is trauma coaching. Melissa has a passion for working with individuals that are reclaiming their lives after trauma due to her personal experiences.

Melissa was widowed at the early age of 34. He husband died of kidney cancer. As she had experienced childhood sexual abuse, the trauma of her husband's illness and death was debilitating for many years. She is a native of South Carolina. Currently, she resides in Knoxville, Tennessee. She is the proud mother of two sons and feels that raising them to feel emotionally safe in such an insecure world is her greatest accomplishment.

https://www.linkedin.com/in/melissa-tyler-todd-41467339/

COACHING A DYSFUNCTIONAL TEAM

Rachel Coucoulas

When I decided to get my coaching certificate, I did it because I wanted to effectively support the sales force I was hired to train and consult. I had no idea how coaching would make such an impactful difference with an entire branch office that was displaying dysfunctional behaviors in many aspects. Before I begin, I will describe attributes missing in this dysfunctional team. There are many characteristics of a functional team and for this exercise, I will highlight the four traits that I found missing in the branch which is the center of this story.

ATTRIBUTES OF A FUNCTIONAL TEAM

Communication: I think the most important part of any successful team is clear, open, transparent communication. I challenge the statement "Knowledge is Power" when it comes to working as a team because the importance of communication supersedes the importance of knowledge. How is success possible without all the information? With good communication, each team member knows and understands the status of the situation along with the steps to achieve a successful end goal. Good communication provides the opportunity to know the information that has a direct impact on what is being done.

Trust: When it comes to working together there must be trust between coworkers. It is simple; if you trust the person you are working with everything moves quickly and efficiently. Instead of wasting time double checking and seeking reassurance, you know that what you expect to get done, gets done. To illustrate the point, think about it this way: there are many people you like, and you may not trust them yet or vice versa. In the workplace this is most commonly either because you do not know them very well or you have observed a lack of follow through. In return, there are some people you trust implicitly because you have seen their follow-through and you may not like them.

> *It is simple; if you trust the person you are working with everything moves quickly and efficiently.*

Healthy Tension: If you have a team that is willing to go to bat for what they believe in and challenge the status quo, you will move forward and build a business or strengthen a relationship. I refer to this as healthy tension. For example: a salesperson comes to the operations team with a very large, new client. This new client will be challenging and wants some extra attention that is within the core competencies of the company. The operations team pushes back saying it is too challenging to take on. If the salesperson accepts this response there is a lack of healthy tension and the company will stagnate. Because the client requests are within the core business structure it is the responsibility of the salesperson to push to make the deal happen.

155

Accountability: When everyone on a team is held accountable for their role and identified expectations, then the team is more fully engaged. Accountability is a negative only when a person or a team is not producing. Successful teams understand what is expected and accept being held accountable. For example, I am much more successful on a diet or at the gym when I have someone holding me accountable to my goals. The same applies on the job; when people know the team will hold them accountable they are more likely to follow through on tasks.

THE BACKGROUND STORY

With that said, I will explain with a story about a very talented and dysfunctional team with whom I had the utmost pleasure of working. I learned as much from them as they did from me. Working with this team was one of my most challenging and rewarding experiences so I am happy to share the journey.

While I was working for a national company as the National Sales Trainer and Consultant, I was asked by my boss what I wanted to do in the future. As we discussed possible paths for growth, operations came up in the conversation. He was shocked to know that I was interested in exploring an operations role since I loved sales and had been successful as a sales executive and trainer. I felt the opportunity was potentially ideal to help round my skillset and ultimately make me a better

156

trainer and resource to the team.   What I did not know was that senior leadership had been throwing my name around as the next Regional Operations Manager for one of our territories and this was his way of seeing if I was going to bite.   The next thing I knew I was meeting with the Sr. Vice President of Operations, whom I highly respected and I thought was a little intimidating. My boss explained that these types of moves take some time and I should not get my hopes up; I was really happy where I was and did not have any expectations.   Well, two weeks later I was in New York to work with some new teammates and was told I was meeting with the President for an interview.   What!?   The President explained he was a formality and the Sr. Vice President that suggested me for the position was the decision maker.   Have you ever been in the situation where you did not volunteer for something and knew you could not say no?   I call that volun-told; meet the new Regional Operations Manager.   I was given the amazing opportunity to venture from the safety of sales and join the operations team for an 8-month rotation.

I did have some experience in operations, so the concept was not completely new to me; I knew it was certainly a huge change and one I anticipated being extremely challenging and rewarding. In this position, I oversaw four regions, each region consisting of 2-4 offices.   Each Branch Manager had a team including Schedulers, Recruiters, Nurse Managers, Care Service Providers, and Business Executives.   In total there were 13 offices throughout the region with hundreds of employees and clients.

Since I was from outside the area, I first traveled around with the Vice President of Operations and met all the Branch Managers that were reporting to me. I wanted to get to know them and their business, understand the different challenges each one faced, and learn what strengths they all brought to the table. In addition, I met the team of one branch that did not have a Branch Manager. I thought to myself, what better way to get to know the staff and the responsibilities of the Branch Managers I was be supporting than to jump right in as the acting Branch Manager? After a long conversation with my VP, I did just that.

THE TEAM

As I spent time in the office learning the roles and responsibilities of the individuals on the team, I realized quickly that the team was displaying dysfunctional behaviors. I had stepped into a group of people that were very strong, knowledgeable, and experienced in their respective positions; they were not a team. The extent of the dysfunction became abundantly clear to me when I decided to take on a very challenging client. I knew the team had the capability to take the case. The question was, were they going to work together to create a successful onboarding and positive outcome for the client without imploding?

> *...were they going to work together to create a successful onboarding and positive outcome...?*

The case in question all started when the Regional Sales Manager and Business Executive asked me for special pricing to bring on a new client. The client had limited funds until their long-term insurance kicked in, and no local family support. This was the first challenging case we were bringing on under my watch, and I wanted to be flexible while sticking to the rules and compliance structure we followed. I really had to trust my team to understand the client's circumstances, detail the expectations, and fully execute the plan.

> *I wanted to be flexible while sticking to the rules...*

It was explained to me that the client, Joe (not his real name), was in a rehabilitation facility and was being discharged within the next few days. His estranged daughter was coming from out-of-state for one day to assist with Joe's transfer home. Usually a family member spent a minimum of three days assisting with this type of transition. We were expected to provide an assessment identifying the appropriate level of home care services and find $5000 worth of missing money somewhere in the apartment. In addition, we knew that the apartment was bug infested and required an exterminator plus scrubbing from top to bottom. All this work was being requested by the daughter to be completed within a very short amount of time and on a shoestring budget. Because I knew the strength of my team, I said yes and accepted the case, even with all the red flags (lack of family support, lack of funds, missing money, bug infestation).

I reached out to the daughter to verify her expectations and discuss our initial plan, welcome her to our care family, and introduce myself. Corporately, we referred to this call as the welcome call. This first welcoming call was an interesting experience; there was nothing too welcoming. Unfortunately, the daughter yelled at me for 30 minutes about her poor relationship with her father and the financial strain it placed. Unfortunately, she felt my company was to blame for this situation, so I suggested we not enter into the business relationship of caring for her father. She said it was too late and that she was stuck with us. Looking back now, I can tell you she was very lucky to be stuck with us.

Following what the team considered normal procedure, the Regional Sales Manager and the Business Executive presented me with the business paperwork. I reviewed the paperwork and then handed it to the Clinical Director and the clinical team working the case. There was nothing normal about this procedure. There was no direct communication between the sales team and the clinical team regarding client details and case information. It was explained to me by the clinicians that the sales team did not know anything about what the clinical team did and therefore their input was unnecessary. In addition, the sales team explained that the clinical team consistently turned down all the cases they signed and therefore left it to the manager to address and hopefully say yes. Ah ha, a trust, healthy tension, and communication issue arose.

I discussed the details I received from the sales team and what I understood to be the client situation with the clinical team. I did receive pushback because of the red flags and challenges; as we discussed the issues in more detail and acknowledged their strengths and capability to achieve success for this client, we devised a plan together. Because I am not clinically trained, I relied on the Social Worker, Registered Nurse, and the Clinical Director to follow proper compliance rules and to move the case forward. While the clinical team was working outside the office, I was talking with the operations team regarding the type of caregiver we were looking for and the skill set. Again, realizing the lack of communication between what the sales team uncovered, what the clinical team planned, and the required information for the operations team to find the best caregivers to staff the case gave me cause for concern.

Once the team had an outline of the plan we went to work. We had the home exterminated and cleaned, removed the dead bugs, scrubbed the apartment, and located $3,000 of the supposed missing $5,000. We transported Joe home from the rehabilitation center, created a care plan through the assessment information, filled his prescriptions, and scheduled a caregiver to help him stay safe and happy at home. Overall, this experience was a success. Joe was in a clean home, had his proper medications, and had a caregiver to supervise him for a few hours a day.

Through the entire process, I watched and listened to this dysfunctional team argue and bicker rather than work together and support each other. There was a clear lack of effective communication with some people having correct information, others with incorrect, and some left out of the loop entirely. Various forms of communication were used: some were texting, some used email, some talked on the phone, and others met in person. There were numerous telephone calls coordinating all aspects of the case and some face to face meetings. It was all very disorganized with no clear leader, process, or verification of information. It seemed as though they were focused on their own individual success. They did not trust one another, held back important details, and were quick to assume teammates were unable or failing to perform their jobs appropriately. At the same time, they seemed content to watch others fail. I was extremely concerned because professionalism was lacking and, more importantly, our job was to take care of the elderly, those that were unsafe alone or unable to fully care for themselves. If we didn't work together someone could get hurt. I had a team that looked like this, three circles independent of each other.

In reality, success meant building a team that looked like this, three circles coming together for a common good.

What was I to do?   Start Coaching.

What was I to do?   Start Coaching.

COACHING FOR COLLABORATION

I decided to call a meeting with the team.   I explained to the team that we were going to work on communication skills and go through a team coaching exercise.   I asked everyone to think about their part in starting any new case.   I asked how best to communicate their information and to whom to communicate that information to be successful.   I also asked them to think about their role in the onboarding process of a new client and their expectations of teammates.   By the end of the meeting, it was my hope that we communicate more effectively, understand each person's role and responsibility, and trust that they were capable.   We were also to discuss healthy tension and how best to support each other through accountability and collaboration.

I took measures prior to the meeting to make sure that our distractions were limited. For example, I asked my other branch managers to handle our calls until the meeting was over. When the team arrived, I paid strict attention to how they interacted, how they spoke with each other, who continued using their phones during the meeting, where they sat, and whom they sat near. I took note of who brought food to share with others and who came with just their notebooks or paperwork. Just watching the team gave me a sense of who was likely to be open from the beginning and who was likely to remain closed-minded. This process helped me to see where tension and potential trust issues were likely between team members, who felt accepted, and who felt like they did not belong.

Since I was new to the team it was important to set some ground rules. I made it clear in the beginning that the purpose of the meeting was so that the team work more effectively together to produce better outcomes for our clients. To do this meant we all be open, honest, fair, respectful, and positive. We anticipated addressing serious challenges during our time together and only through their skill, expertise, knowledge, and commitment were we going to create a strong team. I have to say it was not all roses and rainbows, and there were negative nellies. I decided this was not going to derail the session.

The steps I took to address what I considered to be the primary challenges were first to acknowledge the challenges, communication, and teamwork. I opened this up for discussion with the team and they quickly agreed to engage in the conversation.

Next, we started with the easiest challenge to make progress and used that momentum to tackle the harder challenges. The group easily agreed communication was an issue, so as a group we identified four types of communication we were using:

1. Face-to-face meetings
2. Telephone calls
3. E-mail
4. Text

Each person was asked to explain which style of communication they preferred and why. It was surprising how much interaction there was between the team members regarding forms of communication. It was not surprising to me that they all had very differing opinions. Some felt there were too many emails causing data to be lost. Some liked texting because it was quick and to the point. Others felt that everything was best done face-to-face or over the phone. Clearly, it made sense to come up with a plan to create a path of clear, consistent, and effective communication. I facilitated this portion of the meeting with the intent of moving the group to a place of collaboration and accountability. I started with coaching questions:

- How does your style of communication affect the person with whom you are communicating?
- What will be the best way to share the information you have so that it is best received by your teammates?
- What is your responsibility for sharing the information?
- What is the best way to hold you accountable for acknowledging receipt of and sharing information?

Now that we were looking at this as a process between teammates, the ideas of communication preferences started to shift from an individual opinion to a more collaborative agreement on the best way to communicate. In the end, we came to some conclusions and agreed to the following:

1. Face-to-face meetings held weekly to verify that all team members had the same information about current, new, and potential clients.
2. Telephone calls were best when trying to arrive at an agreement or find a solution.
3. Emails were best to provide group information about the facts of the cases.
4. Text to be used only when an individual wanted a specific piece of information.

In addition to discussing how to communicate, the group also identified who receive what information. We agreed to verify that those impacted by the information be included. It was during this time that the group began talking about overlapping roles during the onboarding process. They realized that often people were left out of the loop unintentionally because the one sharing the information did not make the connection as to why the information they possessed was important to their peer. What emerged was a clearer understanding of the roles, responsibilities, and accountability of each team member.

During the session, I focused on my role as a coach, empowering the team to discuss what worked best for them. This engaged them to put the policies and procedure they preferred in place.

> *This engaged them to put the policies and procedure*
> *they preferred in place.*

While we had positive momentum, I thought it best to press forward. The next challenge was to get this group of professionals to start acting as a team instead of individuals or independent groups.

For this exercise, I reviewed the case of Joe and his daughter. I wanted to use a real scenario to speak to directly and use the best practices of specific communication we had just created. I also used the group coaching method of $+/\Delta$ (plus/delta, the process of reviewing what went well $+$ and what to change Δ). I use this process because it keeps the team away from the blame game when identifying struggles. We reviewed what did we did well and what to change to promote a cohesive team. I was also certain this process had the potential to highlight the trust issues that seemed to linger amongst the group.

I started with the Business Executive asking just those questions, what worked well and what to change. I specifically stated 'we' instead of 'you' because we were all members of the team working to support each other in their respective positions. All team members were invited to join the discussion.

In the beginning, I noticed how each person acted individually and took some responsibility for themselves and their position. Some were very quick to judge and point out what was wrong with teammates and processes. Some supported each other while bringing down others. It got a little heated for sure; it was certainly cathartic.

As we went through the process for each member of the team, I started to see a change in the way they were acting towards one another. As we talked through what worked well, individuals started supporting and identifying all the positive things. When we then asked what to change, it was about identifying how the other teammates could have helped. They were actually offering their assistance and knowledge to each other. They were realizing the importance of every member of the team.

The team started coming together. We were finding ways to understand each person's part in the onboarding of a client. We started to understand the importance of holding each other accountable and the success that it brings. We reviewed the communication process which included how to communicate as well as when and what to communicate.

I had believed this was going to be a positive experience, and even with that the results of this session exceeded my expectations.

After the meeting ended, I was followed back to my office by one of my team members. This individual had been one of the most negative team members. I was very surprised by the outpouring of positive feedback regarding the meeting. This person indicated that this type of leadership, communication, and open forum was exactly what the branch had been missing. They felt they now had the opportunity to be understood and share knowledge freely. As we spoke, there was a knock at the door. Another employee wanted to talk and shared much of what the first person had stated. The openness and joint collaboration was bringing the team together. The idea of understanding what each person's challenges were and being a part of the solution was empowering.

What I learned through this exercise and am so happy to share with you is: when employees take ownership, they are empowered. When they are clearly held accountable to responsibilities and goals, they feel accomplished. When people are empowered and feel accomplished they are successful. When teammates trust each other, there is a natural openness to communication and healthy tension becomes a positive tool. When all the components of communication, trust, healthy tension, and accountability are combined, you have success. Through the identification of these traits and positive coaching, we proved this to be an effective solution to team growth.

> *When people are empowered and feel accomplished they are successful.*

Rachel Coucoulas, CMC, is the founder of Empowered Coaching and Consulting. EC&C focuses on coaching for sales performance, operational efficiencies, and corporate collaboration. Rachel coaches executives in the areas of referral development, professional relationship building, and successful closing skills. With a passion for sales and an energetic approach to identifying root causes, she collaboratively works with individuals and groups to overcome hurdles and achieve success.

As a coach and educator Rachel has married her experience in sales and operations to develop the unique professional relationship building methodology known as HECK™, Help, Easy, Care, Know. This proven method is used to coach individuals and teams through the professional relationship development process to increase referrals, sales, and revenue.

Rachel received both her Certified Professional Coach and Certified Master Coach form the Center for Coaching Certification. She is a Mentor with the Center for Innovation and Entrepreneurs in connection with University of North Carolina Wilmington. A native New Yorker, she moved to North Carolina in 2013 with her family where she is enjoying the warm weather, fishing, and beautiful Topsail Island.

www.EmpoweredCC.com

AN AUTHENTICITY GUIDE FOR THE NEW COACH

Necie Black

I'm naturally a fixer. When family and friends came to me for advice, I was happy to give a variety of solutions. I hated to see anyone struggling or unhappy, so I wanted to fix their problems and make everything better. A willingness to make a difference made coaching an appealing business opportunity. I gladly accepted the responsibility to make sure every client had the answers they sought, applause for what they were doing right, and fixing for what was wrong. As a newbie, I desired to be perfect and stand out amongst coaches who had been in the industry for years. I mean, when you are a new kid on the block you have little credibility, few clients, and certainly little to no following. What I was mistaken about was the misconception surrounding the meaning of professional coaching and that required me to do a bit of research. I found that unlike sports coaches and the like, professional coaches are not intended to be fixers; we are meant to explore perspectives and support a client discovering their own answer. Clearly, my view on what being a coach meant was way off-base and I quickly saw the importance of becoming certified. I learned how embracing the authentic spirit of coaching helps you maintain professionalism, integrity, adhere to a code of ethics, and create a great experience for your client. Some things are learned by trial and error, and this guide shares three of the most important lessons I learned as a new coach.

173

Let me start with a story. "What in the world have I gotten myself into?" This question played over in my mind as I listened to a client complain about how things weren't working between us and she needed answers for her business. I wanted to give her a solution, pray with her, or say something marvelous to help her believe everything would be alright. Instead, I had no insight or strategically formed questions to deepen our conversation. I grew uncomfortable and could feel the blood rise to the top of my scalp. "A coach does not give solutions and we don't give opinions," I warned myself. I continued to flip through my coaching binder filled with weeks of training material. "I can do this! I CAN do this," as my thoughts raced. This was not how a coaching call should go. "Just tell me what to do Necie," she said sarcastically, and I quickly scanned my brain for something brilliant to ask. Exhausted and only 15 minutes into the call, I conceded. It wasn't until the call ended did I face the truth that I lost my courage and had done Shari a disservice by not holding to what I knew was the right thing to do.

Shari was one of my first clients after going through master coaching certification. Paying clients were hard to come by as a newbie coach and I valued every single one. Few prospective clients knew me and I had no references. My certification gave me credibility as I began to build a following on social media. Having a paying client made me feel like a legitimate coach and I still think of Shari and our brief time together. I have spent many moments replaying our sessions in my head, the advice I gave, and how our relationship might have been handled differently. I remember being confidently prepared with notes and scripts and strategically placed questions stuck to my laptop. I knew what to ask and arranged verbiage to keep our sessions on track. Yes, I had a plan and in spite of being nervous, I felt our first session went well. Shari seemed pleased albeit a bit reserved. "Maybe she's still feeling me out," I thought, so I wasn't too concerned.

By our third session something was definitely off. It felt different from the beginning of the call. We began with small talk and I asked about her week and what she wanted to focus on for the day. There was a longer than usual silence and I could feel the knot forming in my stomach. I kept quiet to allow space for her ponder. Shari released a deep sigh and shared how she didn't feel she was making progress since we started coaching together. My heart sank as I listened to her elaborate on what she felt was lacking in my performance. Were there signs from previous sessions I overlooked? Had I not asked the right questions? What about the comments she made about previous coaching experiences that I chose not to address? We both came from a similar entrepreneurial space where titles of trainer, consultant, and mentor were synonymous with coach. It sounded jazzier to say I'm a "this or that" coach and made getting clients easier because you provided strategies a client could follow. Now, I'm not knocking anyone's strategy, I'm suggesting what works for one client may not work for another, so following someone else's strategy for your goals can alter the results you expected to achieve. I wanted to provide a different coaching experience, believing people achieve what they really want faster by developing their own strategies.

> *...believing people achieve what they really want faster*
> *by developing their own strategies.*

The more Shari spoke the more insecure I became. I imagined her leaving a bad review or spreading word of her dissatisfaction. Would I lose business before getting started? I felt ineffective that I didn't live up to her expectation and conceded to the pressure. I had asked Shari what she wanted from me and then answered every question she asked. I gave advice based on my experiences, told her what she could improve, and what I'd do if I were in her situation. The tone of her voice raised and the sound of her fingernails striking the keyboard rang in my ears. The more excited she became, the more I told her what to do. While pleased that Shari now seemed happy, my heart weighed heavy. I've been there before and knew what it felt like to do something I believed was wrong. Honestly, I wanted to earn the money and didn't want to lose a client, so my mind justified every excuse to defy my ethical standards. I felt horrible. Was this feeling worth a dollar? No, it was not.

I couldn't wait for the call to end as my thoughts turned toward our remaining appointments. Truth be told, our coaching partnership ended the moment I meandered away from coaching. It officially ended at our fourth session. We discussed adjusting the contract for me to become her consultant, but in the end I wasn't the person best suited for what she wanted. I was relieved actually, and not in a place where I felt comfortable or confident enough to start over with her as a client. I recognized the lesson in maintaining integrity and a higher level of mental wellness from the start of a coaching relationship. *Ugh!* Shake my head at myself. I vowed not to find myself in this position again, sacrificing what was right for the sake of keeping or gaining another client.

GETTING BACK ON TRACK

Ending the relationship with Shari was the first step towards getting back to honoring me and my business. For a few months following my engagement with her, I was consumed with thoughts of how easily a coaching session can take turn in the wrong direction. I didn't feel ready to take on another client and depended on other ways to earn income. Although I continued to network, I avoided conversations with promising clients because I felt unqualified. I beat myself up quite a bit with guilt and questioned my ability to live up to the title I'd earned during certification. This negative mindset made me consider giving up coaching altogether. Then one day I met a coach who had a similar experience with a client. We talked about challenges new coaches face, including attracting ideal clients and how to change the narrative around coaching misconceptions. It was refreshing to openly share how one session gone awry affected my confidence. I desperately wanted this conversation and began to see that I was not as alone as I felt. There were other coaches who had been where I was in that moment.

The ability to discuss the disappointment, without fear of judgment, gave me the courage to move forward in my business. Isn't it funny how one conversation can change your perspective? Imagine feeling alone, as if no one understands the challenges you face as a new kid on the block. Imagine feeling unqualified, then meeting someone who affirms and helps you remember why you began coaching in the first place. I forgave myself, focused on what I was qualified to do, and relied on the strength of my character, passion for coaching, and contributions that are uniquely me. Becoming a member of the International Coach Federation certainly put me on the right track with an ethical and integrity-based foundation. I am comfortable knowing I won't always get it right, and that the value I am capable of providing keeps me excited and forging ahead.

Earlier, I mentioned three key lessons I learned about honoring yourself, the client, and adhering to the authentic spirit of coaching. The keys are: 1. Relax and be yourself, 2. Stay true to your niche, and 3. Share forever tools. Let's explore them.

1. RELAX AND BE YOURSELF

Many new, and I venture to say, seasoned coaches have at one time or another felt the call to focus on their performance. In this day and time of quick fixes and microwaved solutions, the pressure for a newbie coach to be an instant expert creates unnecessary anxiety. For example, have you ever felt uncomfortable with silence, as if you should be doing or saying something during that silence? Thought-provoking questioning is perfect for clients to reflect, and with too much silence we feel pressured to say something. This scenario plays out often for new coaches, as we eagerly jump in with our own words. Interrupting silence can keep the client from travelling the direction of their own thoughts. It shifts the focus to your performance and away from listening. By injecting your words, you can appear to be dismissive of the client's thoughts or words and lead them down a path you chose. Be patient with the length of time it takes a client to respond. Relax and be present in the silence, knowing that you are serving them, and listen with a curiosity to fully understand your client.

This was one of my first lessons; accepting that it was both unnecessary and inappropriate to have the answer. To relax and let the client be the main attraction freed me from attempting to perform. To show up genuine and curious to explore with them is what we are charged with doing. Clients know what is best for their life, even if they are momentarily stuck, confused, or fearful. It is our responsibility as coaches to help them uncover and formulate their own path forward.

Developing your unique style, personality, and approach to the coaching process is what will make you stand out as you build your business.

When thinking about authenticity, the words genuine and real often come to mind. The unspoken benefit, especially for new coaches, is quickly being comfortable with challenging conversations, and approaching them with openness and transparency. Because every client is different, being able to maintain your poise and professionalism will strengthen the relationship. This means if a client is frustrated, you can remain calm. If a client expresses anger, you can constructively walk them through it, without taking any of it personally. You put clients at ease by being at ease with yourself. I think about emotional intelligence and the ability to manage your emotions and those of others. While I am unconvinced any of us can control the emotions of others, I do believe managing our own emotions and responses has a huge influence in effectively coaching a client in managing their emotions. Managing the emotions of others is about accepting and working with their emotions without taking them on. This is important in coaching and in everyday living. It makes sense to self-assess or look within for unchecked emotions that negatively affect your perception and presence. Remember the range of emotions I felt with Shari? I became anxious when facing situations that didn't go according to plan. Knowing how you are prone to think, feel, and behave, in any situation makes getting to the root of your frustration easier and bouncing back much quicker.

> *Knowing how you are prone to think, feel, and behave,*
> *in any situation makes getting to the root of your frustration*
> *easier and bouncing back much quicker.*

As a new coach, there are a few things that can create self-inflicted anxiety. I am guessing you will have moments when you feel inadequate, ineffective, and unprepared. There will likely be times when you are afraid of not knowing what you don't know or wonder if you miscalculated your calling. Let me be clear: uncertainty often rears its ugly head, if even for a second. It is okay because you are human. Uncertainty is normal; keep serving others in the capacity you desire. Instead of fear causing you to show up inauthentically for the sake of being an expert, choose to do something productive with any negative energy you experience. You will find yourself achieving more each day. Here are a few tips to focus on as you grow your business:

- Remember. No one starts out a seasoned coach, just like a baby isn't born walking. Get practice clients by offering a discount so you can hone your skill. Family and friends may be willing to support in this way – make it real by charging a nominal fee in exchange for the value you provide. Doing so will help you become comfortable in the coaching process.

- There are more than enough people in the world who seek coaching, so build relationships with other coaches and share experiences, resources, and tried-and-true practices. Stay up-to-date on industry shifts and culture changes. Be open to learning new techniques that will benefit your clients.

- Have faith in you. Trust in your skillset. Believe you are well-equipped, prepared, and possess everything required to help clients create a positive transformation for their life. Affirm what you want to see happen in your business; affirmations are wonderful in keeping your focus positive.

> *Have faith in you.   Trust in your skillset.*

Authenticity is real, so stay true to who you are, where you are at, and your abilities to serve. Have faith in your abilities as you continue to learn and grow into a higher level of coaching. Be real, honest, and true to who you are, at your core. The world wants coaches who confidently provide a safe, non-judgmental, and empowering space for client self-discovery. So, exhale, relax and have faith in you. Open the door for grace and ease to guide your path of becoming a sought-after leader in your field.

2. Stay True to Your Niche

Imagine going to a gym to purchase the membership you believe will help you achieve your weight goal. You are a bit nervous because you haven't had a good work out in ages and you are unsure what to expect. You've tried do-it-yourself exercises, and your results are limited. With trepidation you arrive at the gym and are greeted by someone who asks about your goals. This person listens, ask what you have tried before, and guides you around the facility. They reassure you that everyone gets stuck and applaud you for seeking help. When the tour is complete, you are confident this gym is the right path to a healthy and active lifestyle. This scenario is similar to someone looking for the right coach. Whether a coach, or a gym, clients deserve to work with someone who cares and can help them achieve the results they desire.

For a new coach, getting your first few clients can be a tad daunting. There are expectations for both the coach and client that must be clearly understood well in advance of the first session. In fact, the conversation leading to an introduction call is an opportunity to lay a foundation of genuine trust. How so? By being clear on the type of clients you work with and the scope of coaching you provide. It is having a niche or specialty. For example, if you are a career coach, you may have the ability to coach someone in a different area. Ask yourself the pros and cons of moving into different areas. Ask yourself what you want to be known for in the coaching profession. Finding my niche was my second important lesson as a new coach. When I completed certification, I thought I could coach anybody through anything. How very naïve of me to think my services were a fit for everyone. I soon realized not every client was my ideal client, and I did not even want to coach certain people. I had the right to choose. If you aren't sure what type of coach you want to be, hire a coach to help you figure it out. Yes, every coach ideally has a coach (and possibly a consultant too) to help you work out the details of your business. As you begin coaching, you will narrow the focus of your services even more.

Being a jack-of-all-trades type of coach, i.e. someone who coaches everyone while specializing in nothing, sends mixed messages when you are marketing for potential clients. If what you want is to build a reputation as a (fill in the blank) coach, stay true to your specialty during initial conversations with promising clients. When chatting with someone who wants to hire you and what they want is outside your specialization, gladly refer them to another coach who can assist them. People appreciate when you are clear about who you serve, and you respect everyone's time. You become a valued resource for future opportunities as you show up authentically to your calling. Honesty and trust go a long way in building rapport with other coaches in the profession. Stay true to your niche, be comfortable with who you are, and the ideal client will show up.

Once a promising client is interested in learning more about you and your services, establish a solid foundation with an introduction call. An introduction call is a 20-30-minute conversation with a hopeful client to introduce them to your coaching experience. As a newbie coach, I skipped over this very important step in the process, several times, and before I knew what happened I was in a contract with someone who didn't fully understand the process. Only some clients will read the details of a coaching agreement, so go a step further and discuss it with them so boundaries and expectations are clear. The introduction call answers the most pressing client questions, brings ease to closing the deal, and makes onboarding new clients smoother.

2. SHARE FOREVER TOOLS

The last thing I want is a forever client who comes back to me for coaching around the same issues. I had a client who had great progress during our sessions and left with a documented plan in place when our contract ended. Several months later she called and admitted she was having the same issue, with a different person, and was stuck with what to do next. This made me wonder how effective I had or had not been with helping her see all she accomplished. At that point I decided to share and discuss some of the tools I use during our sessions, with the client's permission of course. The old saying is true:

give me a fish and I am fed for today; if you teach me how to fish I will know how to feed myself throughout my life. Having easy-to-apply tools helps the client to walk themselves through the same or similar situations in the future, and it builds their confidence and their ability to self-manage.

Tool #1 – Be Present: Have a quiet moment in advance of your session so your mind will be focused and engaged when you meet with the client. As a prelude to your sessions, let those around you know you are to be undisturbed for the duration. I use a 15-minute benchmark to ensure there's quiet space before and after a meeting. Center yourself, stop multitasking, and silence cell phones, computers, and reminder notifications. Remove any other distractions that might interrupt your client's time. These are the sort of things I share with clients, so they can recreate a calming space whenever they feel it will help them relax or focus on day-to-day responsibilities.

Side note: Admit when you are ill instead of pushing through a coaching session. This happened to me with an early morning call after I was sick all night. Instead of rescheduling, I wanted to be a trooper and have the call anyway. It took the client to say she was rescheduling because obviously I was distracted, and she wouldn't get the full benefit of our session. She was right. It dawned on me that not only could my client have done something else with her time, I did not exercise proper self-care by rescheduling in advance. It is important to recognize when

186

to exercise self-care, model self-care for others, and show up your best self when you are better.

Tool #2 – Be Curious: Your coaching time becomes much more productive when the atmosphere is conducive to exploration. The client is feeling you out and you co-create a safe place to be open, provide observations, and engage with a powerful line of questioning. Be direct with your questions and resist beating around the bush. You are their coach, not their buddy, so use the trust you create to take the client deeper into the ideas and challenges surrounding their goals. Make sure to rephrase or summarize what you believe you heard the client say to ensure your understanding and, more importantly, their clarity. Give them the opportunity to confirm or correct. Be open to any correction a client makes and continue to engage and clarify. There is unspoken validation in being heard and your client will appreciate a genuine interest as they make progress.

It is okay to admit when you are unfamiliar with terminology or a reference the client makes, so if it is relevant be okay with asking. Once, a client used an abbreviation I was familiar with, except it meant one thing for her and another for me. I waited a few minutes before asking her to clarify, which threw off our conversation when she circled back. For clarity's sake I now ask, "What do you mean by x, y, and z?" Even if you are familiar with their terminology, asking is an authentic step to ensure you understand from the client's perspective and gets them sharing even more. Demonstrating curiosity, and exploring with open-ended questions, lays a foundation for clients to grow comfortable asking for clarity in their day-to-day relationships. They learn what curiosity looks and feels like in a safe coaching space, and it builds their inquisitive confidence for deeper insight and exploration with others.

Tool #3 – Be Courageous: Be unafraid to go there with the client and be willing to ask the tough questions. Avoiding sensitive matters may give the client permission to avoid what is uncomfortable. Resist beating around the bush or overly explaining your questions; instead make them short, clear, and to the point. Now, I have had clients who were master deflectors and it felt like I was playing a game of tennis. I asked questions and the client asked questions back. I asked them to elaborate, and they go off topic. It can be uncomfortable, so relax and shift when the client shifts to stay in the moment with them. Acknowledge the shift and explore it. Gently guide them back to topic, if it is what they desire. Doing so keeps the client focused on uncovering and manifesting their solutions much faster.

It takes courage to walk through the up-and-down moments of a client session, helping them face what is uncomfortable and work through it. Coaching sessions are a safe place that strengthen the client's confidence and builds their fortitude for breaking through challenges in their day-to-day life, and certainly for obstacles that lie well ahead of them. Courage is a wonderful tool for all of us to utilize. As we overcome our own struggles, we become resilient in dealing with them, and can experience quicker breakthroughs for ourselves and those we serve.

Being bold enough to be yourself is sometimes all it takes to make a difference. When you are comfortable with who you are and create an authentic space for others to openly share the most intimate parts of their life, it sets the stage for real transformation to take place. Your authenticity permit clients to explore deeper, empowering a shift in perspective and a pathway for change. You win too! You become a better coach, a better person with a happier, richer, and fuller life of your own. What a blessing you are, with a wonderful gift to share!

In this moment, know that you are celebrated for your choice to make the world better than you found it. From one coach to another on this journey, we want you and others like you. Let us stand in solidarity, shoulder to shoulder, as we effect change one client at a time.

> *Let us stand in solidarity, shoulder to shoulder,*
> *as we effect change one client at a time.*

Cheers to you for showing up authentically and creating greater impact and influence in the lives of others both personally and professionally.

As a coach and speaker, Necie Black helps high-performing and over-worked women become a priority in their life. Empowering women is Necie's passion. After two failed marriages, she persevered through low self-esteem, anchored her faith in God, and now helps other women love and accept who they are, manifest their authentic self, and create the lifestyle they desire. To honor her passion, Necie published, *Self-Approved; A Guide for Authentic and Purposeful Living* with a follow-up journal, *Affirmations in Action.*

Equally passionate about synergy in the workplace, after 30+ years in corporate, Necie founded Lyfe Smarts LLC., a training platform designed to help organizations cultivate stronger relationships with the effective use of Strengths.

Necie is a Strengths Strategy Coach, Certified People Acuity Specialist™, and a Strengths Strategy for Optimal Performance Facilitator. She is a Certified Professional and Master Coach and is a member of the ICF-Arkansas/Oklahoma chapter.

Necie holds a Master's in Business and serves her community as Board Development Chair with Dress for Success Oklahoma, a non-profit organization providing women a network of support, professional attire, and tools to thrive in work and life.

www.NecieBlack.com

TRUE CHANGE AT 180 DEGREES

Kristen Hess-Winters

Most of us consider change in our lives inevitable. On the other hand, change in who we are is an entirely different story. We can look at ourselves and see room for improvement. We can see those areas or characteristics where we want to improve. What about when we must change because otherwise there will be a negative impact in our lives? That change sometimes is the hardest because it is driven externally or is only to avoid a consequence. When the change is because you want it, that is where you have the greatest opportunity. This chapter will talk about that change and what is required for a complete 180-degree turn. You will learn to start on a different path, in a way that it will become permanent. By sharing my own experiences with this subject, I will provide insight on what can be a challenging process and one that can be rewarding once you fully experience True Change at 180 Degrees.

> *When the change is because you want it, that is where you have the greatest opportunity.*

In this chapter I will write the word you and that you may be a client or someone you know. I will also include myself in many statements with the word we because I have learned much of this through personal experience and we are on the journey together.

192

MINDSET: FIXED TO GROWTH

Your mindset sets the path and pace in which you can move forward. The mind is one of the most powerful things you possess, and your mind controls your life and your actions.

People have so many different mindsets. Examples include social, growth, fear, lazy, dreamer, follower, confident, angry, and so on. Think about people you know, reflect on your own mindset, and observe the impact of these different mindsets.

For this chapter, I want to concentrate on the growth and fixed mindset because I think that with all the mindsets that are out there, these two are the ones encompass all the others. One will keep you from moving forward and the other will empower you to excel.

For our purposes, the definition of mindset is a predetermined way of thinking about something or someone that guides our understanding and response to circumstances. So, we are already predisposed to a fixed mental attitude. That mental attitude will make responses almost automatic which in turn is what usually keeps us from the change we want and our goals.

When you desire change, first change the mindset you have been using for the way things are now. This will be one of the most important and challenging steps in the process. It also must be the first thing to happen to truly change your path. Your belief system affects your mindset. What you believe is also a factor in the actions you take. Changing your belief system takes hard work; it is possible. Start by choosing a belief system that is open to listening and accepting the views of others as well as outcomes in those views so that you are naturally empowered to choose your mindset.

The goal is to make the shift because you recognize how much better things will be after the change. Changing your mindset can be intimidating so taking it one step at a time and setting smaller goals to reach the greater goal is a smart way to start. Let us explore smaller goals and ways to set the pace for moving forward. Remember, whatever the pace, if you are moving toward what you want, then you are moving in the right direction.

Fixed: A fixed mindset will keep you where you are now, so let us explore the reasons and what to do about it. With a fixed mindset, you are more likely to avoid challenges which make you grow. You often feel threatened and likely feel defensive. People with fixed mindsets have higher levels of depression and tend to be negative people. When you are looking at it that way, most people will agree that they want a different mindset.

What can we do to alter the fixed mindset? First look within yourself. What are the reasons you have no desire to change your mind? For some it might be because it is part of a core belief and for others it is because it is easier than taking the time to listen to another view or be open to change. When you discover the reason, you can then begin to work through that and get to the core of your fixed thoughts. I truly believe that people develop their fixed beliefs or fixed mindsets based on experiences they have had. Sometimes those experiences are remembered and sometimes it is only a sense of something from childhood. Give time to understanding where your reasons come from and work through those experiences. It takes more than getting up one day and saying, "I am going to change the way I believe." Your instinct will kick in and set up barriers. Dive deep into what caused it and explore whether that is serving you now. Finding a coach that will help you explore this and will be a powerful tool for switching over to a growth mindset. Switching to the growth mindset will give you the power of making your own choices and the reward of feeling free and open to change. Create the space for a fixed mindset to change to a growth mindset.

Growth: The growth mindset is a powerful and rewarding way to think. Being able to listen to other opinions and truly hear someone and their views empowers you to expand personally and professionally.

Sometimes people are fearful of openly listening because they think it means changing core beliefs. Core beliefs remain a part of you for as long as you choose and at the same time you can be open to hearing others too. Hearing and listening to others simply means that you approach things openly for a better evaluation of a different thought process. Take time to notice and think about your reactions or perceptions. When you do that, you begin to be more open-minded and then planned or auto responses begin to change. This will make you more approachable, well grounded, and empowered.

Some people fear that if they allow other opinions to enter their thoughts, that they are being forced to change their mind. This is a myth; the reality is that it empowers you to expand your learning and knowledge by hearing others and viewing things through a different lens. Keeping with your core beliefs can be your constant. Being open to other views empowers you to evaluate a thought and therefore open a door for a change if you find that is appropriate and choose to change.

Being in the growth mindset will empower you to continue learning, accept and invite challenges and opportunities, and embrace your weaknesses. A growth mindset will make you a stronger person. Your brain has the ability to change; the real question is whether you are open, willing, or wanting change. Choosing an open mindset will create calm and empowerment that will reward you in so many ways throughout your life.

A growth mindset will make you a stronger person.

THE ABILITY AND WILL TO CHANGE

Once we have decided to change our mindset, what happens when your will gets in the way? The ability to change is in us all. We all have free will and so it is important to think about the role it plays in the process. Your will to do something is the most challenging part. Think about what is takes to motivate you to do something different.

As we explore your ability versus your will, remember the will to do something creates the ability to do it. We tend to go mindlessly about our day and come to the end of the day with no change at all. It is much easier to stay in our patterns than to require more of ourselves. We may say, "I just can't do it." Typically, that is an excuse and a lack of commitment. I read somewhere about a woman who said, "I would love to go to medical school, but it takes seven to ten years and I'll be 50 years old in seven years!" A wise friend responded, "Well, how old will you be in seven years if you don't go?" It's all about perspective and focus. Focus on what you want and then set the plan in motion to accomplish it.

Here are seven things that I think are important to clear a path for the will to access your ability to change.

1. **Examine Your Past Choices**. It is important to look at the choices you have made in the past. How did they affect

your life? What choices will you make moving forward that will get you a different result? How will you make choices now to move toward your goal? What regrets do you have about your past decisions? How can regrets about some choices become a way to learn and make choices for the result you want now? Focus on the positive and use the lessons along the way to guide you towards a positive outcome.

For example, one lesson is that decisions that you make each day will affect the direction in which you are headed. The smallest choice can lead to a bigger choice down the road. Stopping and evaluating each choice for the potential outcome can help you weigh the pros and cons before the decision is made to help you better choose. We are creatures of habit and sometimes we just choose something because it is what you have always done. What if you chose a different way to drive to work one day? What if you chose to drink water instead of juice in the mornings?

Another lesson is that our decisions can make us feel differently. If we are unhappy, then we can choose to do something different. For example, I feel an important decision each day is 30 minutes of me time. Taking 30 minutes to self-reflect, write an affirmation for the day, and think are important parts for our minds to clear and make better choices. Taking this time, in my opinion, will be imperative to changing behavior.

2. **Speak Your Mind Kindly and with Purpose**. Both honesty and learning to speak your mind are important. If you are afraid of saying your thoughts out loud you stay stuck. Speaking what you truly want, feel, or desire is the right thing! To achieve your goals means being courageous and saying them out loud. You will encounter those that misunderstand or misinterpret speaking your mind. Although delivery is to be considered, it is fact that when you speak your mind, you are respecting yourself. You are taking the steps to manage your life and making sure that your interests are heard. When you are heard challenging times will be more bearable because you got to speak your piece. If you fail to speak up, you will have another regret and often it negatively impacts others too. Silence will cause you more stress and that can lead to health issues. A suggestion for delivery is to take a deep breath and count to five before you speak. This will give you the space to bring your thoughts together and deliver in a calm and deliberate way.

3. **Expect Only What People Can Give**. Here's a big one. Don't expect more from people than they can give. Sometimes, others are just not going to give you what you want, and so accept what they can give graciously. If you

do this, you will minimize being disappointed and allowing that disappointment to hold you back from moving forward. We are all human. Expecting of others what you expect of yourself is unrealistic.

We all have different quirks that make us who we are. To enhance awareness of what you can expect, start with those closest to you. For example, my husband, oh how I love him so, drives me crazy sometimes. Every time we are getting ready to leave the house, he decides it is time to clean something. Seriously. He literally will get down on his hands and knees and start wiping the floor! All the while, I am sitting there with our 3-year-old ready to walk out the door. Frustrating; he has done this for years. I have asked him why and he always says he just sees something and prefers to come back to it being done. After 16 years of marriage I have come to expect him to want to take care of what he notices before we walk out the door. I have built time into our process to allow for this part of his routine. It occasionally still gets under my skin of course, except now I rest in the fact that we will be on time. Additionally, I have learned to be grateful as it saves me cleaning it!

It is all about perspectives and most of us have that one thing that gets us biting our tongues. Find a way to embrace those things. How can you make that thing a positive thing for you? How can you change the way you look at it to have a positive affect? How can those frustrations benefit you and your goals? This perspective helps move us forward, so we grow in our ability to see others for who they are, and it ensures our expectations are reasonable and understandable.

4. **Push Yourself**. Push yourself past your comfort zone. Demand more from yourself. If you stay where you are currently, you will fail to challenge yourself and you will fail to reach the next goal. Growth and change come from pushing past our fears and comfort. It is like exercising. If you do the same thing every day and stop when you get to the point of a little pain, you will stay at your current level of strength. It takes a little pain to reach the next level. Use the fear of failing to push forward and make the effort. The failures we endure teach many lessons and those lessons empower us to see how to go forward and do things differently the next time. Failure is an opportunity to learn.

Failures are to be embraced. Each person judges what they think is success and failure. Everyone will view it differently. Stopping and evaluating these setbacks will help us go in a different direction next time. What could I have done differently for a different outcome? What level of control did I have in this situation? If it's something I could not control, how will I make sure to have the control next time? If it is something I control, what am I learning that will make a difference next time? These questions help us evaluate the failure as a lesson and learn from it. Embracing these moments will set you free and empower you to see the big picture, make you humbler, and push past the fear. Remember the next time you will succeed and that will taste even better because you have seen it from the other side.

5. **Be Yourself**. It is a big mistake to compare you or your life with anyone else. Sometimes we feel the compulsion to be like everyone else, or sometimes better. Why? We think it makes us look better. The reality is, few noticed and fewer believed anyway. Stories that are puffed up come across puffed up. People are very intuitive and can see through the fluff.

Being yourself is so rewarding. You will find that others are more accepting because you are genuine. Every person's situation is different, and you rarely truly know how another person is feeling or the life they are living behind closed doors. What you think they have may be way more challenging to them than you realize. Be happy with yourself and focus on what you can do to change your circumstances in a positive way. Being genuine means being authentic. When you are genuine with others, they trust you and accept you naturally. When you accept who you are and display your real self, you will find those you love and are close to will be drawn closer to you naturally. When we give are real it provides a much better perspective and begins the process of self-awareness and self-love.

6. **Be Simple**.   Being simple will go a long way toward empowering you to focus on change.   The less we have of the things that are unnecessary, the more room is made for what is important.

What useless things can you remove from your life?   What will happen to your perspective when those things are removed?   Sometimes we hold on to things because they are familiar.   Staying with things that are familiar is something we instinctively gravitate towards.   When we examine if it is having a positive impact or hindering us, we often find that the removal of that thing will helps us to move forward.   Cleaning out our closets (so to speak) creates room for positive things.

7. **Own Your Mistakes and Choices**.   Owning up to your mistakes and asking for forgiveness is an important part of this process.   It is also important to understand that just because you ask for forgiveness, doesn't mean you will always get it.   Know that is okay.   Sometimes we hurt people so much that it takes time and it may or may not be fully repaired.

I once asked counselor, how long do I have to ask for forgiveness? How long do I have to keep saying I am sorry? His response was compelling. He just simply said, "Until." I sat there trying to process. Then it hit me; until the hurt party is ready to forgive, until they are ready to accept your apology. Until, Until, Until. This is hard and sometimes frustrating for us that have caused the hurt. The other side may or may not be ready to move on. Remember Tip number 3? Expect from others only what they can give. This applies here as well.

Accept that we sometimes cause such harm and hurt that the process for others may take longer. Accept that they may or may not get to the place where they once were and accept the place they can get to or are at now. This will probably be one of the most difficult of the seven tips; I know it was and is for me. It is part of us growing into a better person and learning how our actions affect others by accepting that, even if it goes against what we think makes sense.

Remember that change occurs from being aware of who you are authentically. Embrace you and your feelings. Feel the negative as well as the positive; both have their place, and both empower you to grow and move forward towards a positive outcome.

> *...change occurs from being aware of who you are authentically.*

THE IMPLEMENTATION AND EXECUTION OF REAL CHANGE

So now that we have changed our mindset, discovered how ability and our own will to do something affects our success, and have tips for moving forward, we can implement all of it to fully live a changed life. A life that is ever growing, enhanced, and transformed. Continue to set new goals for yourself. Maintain the focus on things that you can change. Empower yourself to fail and be ok with it because failures will give you lessons for moving forward. Plan for your future while living in the moment of today. Demand more of yourself every day and if you are afraid of something, face it head on! Remember that happiness is different than what we call pleasure. Pleasure is a moment in time. Truly being happy is accepting you as you are, doing what you love.

Surround yourself with people that you aspire to be like. They will help you get to where you want to go. Clear space for the things that support you, your goals, and your life. Most importantly, examine, accept, and push forward.

I will leave you with 9 Mark Twain's quotes (shared with the permission publicly provided online). I put them in this order intentionally. I think they are wise and sum up this chapter nicely.

1. "A man cannot be comfortable without his own approval."

2. "Age is an issue of mind over matter. If you don't mind, it doesn't matter.

3. "Humor is mankind's greatest blessing. Against the assault of laughter nothing can stand."

4. "Anger is an acid that can do more harm to the vessel in which it is stored than to anything on which it is poured."

5. "Don't go around saying the world owes you a living. The world owes you nothing. It was here first."

6. "A person with a new idea is a crank until the idea succeeds."

7. "Drag your thoughts away from your troubles... by the ears, by the heels, or any other way you can manage it."

8. "The best way to cheer yourself up is to try to cheer somebody else up."

And my personal favorite:

9. "Twenty years from now you will be more disappointed by the things that you didn't do than by the ones you did so throw off the bowlines. Sail away from the safe harbor. Catch the trade winds in your sail. Explore. Dream. Discover."

So, G.E.T. Into Focus!

Grow. Empower. Transform.

 **Kristen Hess-Winters** is the Principal Broker of InFocus Real Estate Group and a Certified Professional Coach at G.E.T. In Focus Coaching.

Helping others reach their potential is a passion. Kristen is a licensed Real Estate Broker and owner of both InFocus Real Estate Group and G.E.T. In Focus Coaching. Helping individuals empower themselves as she watches the transformation is invigorating.

Kristen is a mother of 4 children, Kara, Maegan, Zach, and Aleeyah. She is married to the love of her life, Don, and holds her faith very close as she knows she is where she is today because of God. She owns a gourmet marshmallow company called The Edible Cloud and enjoys making those sweet puffs in her spare time. She actively supports Stepping Stones, giving a portion of all profits from all her companies to their organization.

Awards and Certifications:
Graduate of the CABR Leadership Academy 2016
OAR President's Sales Club Award 2017, 2018
CABR Circle of Excellence 2017
Five Star Award Recipient 2018
Best of Cincinnati Award for InFocus Real Estate Group 2017
Best of the East Award for InFocus Real Estate Group 2018

PERFECTLY POISED TO PROSPER

Renee Hutcherson Lucier

WHAT IS DRIVING YOUR BUS?

Often, in the drama of our lives, we allow our thoughts, self-talk, negative experiences, and emotions free reign within our being. When we give consent to doubt, fear, and timidity these emotions rise like the steam of our morning coffees through the cracked door of our minds and seize our senses. Our palettes, well, bless them, are completely outmatched. They begin to water and beg to savor the rich, dark chocolate flavor running all thru our favorite coffee drink. And that's it! You are done for the day and you, my friend, were just getting started.

This chapter explores the truth that you are, at this moment, already perfectly poised to prosper. There may be any number of reasons you have yet to step into your greatness. We will look at what may be hindering your prosperity. We will unearth what is giving momentum to this level of thinking that is paralyzing you by examining your thoughts, self-talk, and emotions. We will look behind the mirror to consider other perspectives regarding your missteps, momentary defeats, and failures. Lastly, we will investigate the emotions at play within you to herald the importance of engaging your feelings so that you are in a better position to first determine your best achievable result and then use your emotions to achieve it. My hope is that you grasp how to acknowledge your power during the incredible moments that life hurls your way, and to seize it, exercise control over it, and effectively use it to catapult you forward!

In addition to a whole new process to learn, there will also be an Action Worksheet at the end of the chapter. I recommend that you use it daily to push through the tough moments and unleash your power. Your being is waiting on you. I know you are ready. Whew, look out world! Let's do this!

You are an amazing creation! Already placed within you is the perfect arsenal to defeat every threat that dares to cross your path. Just as a fighter trains to utilize weapons for his triumph, you must too. Become proficient with your power. Unleash your warrior!

Every one of us has a dramatic undertone to our life that we either tune in to, tune out of, or consistently change the channel on. It is a sports announcer or disc jockey that is always at play, day and night, in our minds. This chatter, or self-talk, does everything from perceiving situations to providing opinions, evaluations, motivations, criticisms, and even voicing our unconscious assumptions and beliefs. While our self-talk can be sensible, it can also be destructive, impractical, and quite disadvantageous to the psyche.

When we exert skill to strengthen our ability to perceive why the chatter is being said in our minds, we challenge the negative slant, testing its validity, rationality, and truth, and ultimately replace it with reason, affirmations of power, constructs of goal-directed conviction, and action. It is crucial to be aware of our self-talk to ensure our internal communication is healthy, positive, and beneficial. This self-check has dramatic effects on our performance, empowers us to become more effective, and then inspires others to achieve success for themselves.

To consider the gripping power of self-talk and its detrimental effects, contemplate the likelihood of this occurring at your work. Imagine a small, important meeting with senior managers where the strategy behind an imminent marketing launch is being discussed. This multifaceted operation involves layers of specific action by members of your team and several others. It is imperative that you oversee the completion of each action and report to your senior vice president and the vice presidents of other teams. Inside your head, chatter is playing at a low volume. As the meeting continues, you allow the volume to turn up little by little until finally you can make out exactly what your internal disc jockey is saying. You hate metrics! The last time you were charged with tracking a campaign's marketing efforts, you failed miserably and had to launch a covert salvage operation. Almost everyone in the room knows of the fail. No matter that the covert mission resulted in a surprising success, even more so than the initial projections, you dwell on the fail. You dramatically turn up the volume with each perceived look, imagining awareness of your weakness instead of their simple quest for comprehension. What began in a small space of your mind soon emerged to wreak havoc on your circumstances. As the meeting continued, you turned up the volume on the chatter just a bit more, resisting its distracting and debilitating charge less, until you were present physically in the meeting while mentally you were miles away. What in the world is driving your bus? The answer? Negative self-talk and senseless head chatter. To combat these, chop the chatter, release your will, engage positive emotions of believability, and immediately effect action.

> *...engage positive emotions of believability,*
> *and immediately effect action.*

CHOP THE CHATTER

To utilize the most effective process for harnessing your power, remember these four C's:

1. **Check It.** Consider evidence both for and against what is inside your thoughts. Inquire whether your thoughts are accurate. Determine whether you are making assumptions. Apart from your fears, identify the real situation.

2. **Challenge It.** Instead of believing the chatter inside your head, take the time to understand other ways the situation could be perceived. Uncover significance in

each possibility. Let each resonate within your mind, body, spirit, and emotions in healthy, positive, constructive ways.

3. **Channel It.** Explore the extent of your emotions, which ones are present, why that is, and how they are portraying the situation, perhaps in the worst light. Weigh the best possible outcome against the worst possible one and investigate the likelihood for both. Determine one positive good thing about the circumstance, and then another, and then another. Consider what effect will remain in five years.

4. **Change It.** Pursue a belief system that creates opportunities to empower the essential strengthening that expedites mastery of skills for creativity, goal achievement, conflict resolution, emotional resilience, confidence of abilities, high productivity, and strong, effective leadership. State with detail what is possible based on these criteria.

Instead of allowing negative self-talk to twist the pathway to insight, harness your power and then release your will. To harness your power, it is imperative that you Chop the Chatter. Check what is being said for validity, challenge each negative utterance in your mind by opening up to additional rationales, channel the chatter into a suitable perspective, and then change the unhealthy, negative perception to generate a desirable, beneficial outcome. After attacking the chatter and maneuvering it for productive use, it is essential to declare affirmation statements with certainty and follow up with immediate and appropriate action. Then, immediately and intensely, call forth an emotion of belief and apply appropriate action to seal the deal. Applying these effective strategies for empowering the full release of personal power in the example above means an outcome that is quite different.

Back in the example, imaging you are required to oversee several stages of the project to ensure your team successfully completes each component prior to handing it over to the other teams. Inside your head, you still hate metrics while conceding their importance. As the flourishing, victorious professional that you are, you celebrate each perplexing experience as a revelation of where you want additional strengthening. Instead of hyper focusing on what was previously regarded as the fail, you remind the disc jockey in your head about the value of every single lesson you learned from those marketing challenges and utterly re-sell yourself on the results you will realize through achieving success.

After you completely deconstruct the negative self-talk and refashion it for constructive use, the final steps include affirming everything you aim for, aligning emotions of believability, and immediately stepping into a corresponding action. As a standard:

1. Profess several declarations that validate each positive good thing on the exhaustive list of channeled items.
2. Express the details of what you now strongly believe.
3. Assign the fullness of your emotion and believability.
4. Seal your beliefs with actions that validate your truths.

Each declaration is to be expressed using the words 'I am' and 'I will' to affirm the certainty of the positive occurring. Employing this process, along with avowing the appropriate affirmation statements, conveying full emotion, and activating your belief at every opportunity will effectively release your power over your self-talk and your circumstances.

Consideration of the mistakes experienced previously weighed against the opportunity before you to explore what has been gleaned means your self-talk sounds like this:

- "I <u>am</u> grateful for this incredible opportunity to exemplify my bona fide skill, which has already been proven through countless accomplishments and merits, and <u>will</u> result in another victory today."
- "I <u>am</u> satisfied with my ability to succeed because of every lesson before where I already exemplified mastery which brings me into this moment where I <u>will</u> shine today."
- "I <u>am</u> successful in employing a proven system that combines my achievements, expertise in my field,

natural talent and abilities, as well as the belief I have about the good that I do, and I <u>will</u> triumph today."

An additional strategy to further the process of seizing your thoughts, self-talk, and emotions includes writing yourself a letter with several strategies to create outcomes that you want, as well as accomplishments you hope to achieve. What will be clearly seen as a result is the extent of your motivating and/or debilitating self-talk.

In situations of heightened stress, the degree of creativity, resourcefulness, confidence, and leadership ability that you demonstrate determines your level of effectiveness. It also demonstrates whether you use constructive self-talk, ineffective and dysfunctional self-talk, or are somewhere along the scale in between. As you can imagine, constructive self-talkers possess more desirable qualities as there is a direct correlation with self-talk and the results achieved. Conversely, when someone allows negative chatter to increasingly bring about self-scrutiny and insecurity, their mind becomes paralyzed with anxiety, believing the self-talk that says circumstances are utterly devastating. Instead of utilizing existing incredible creative abilities to bring about solutions to challenges, they will incessantly question their abilities and negate their skills.

To give a workplace example, this leads to becoming fearful of being found an imposter. A highly skilled leader resorts little by little to undermining their own achievements, discounting praise received by others, and shrinking instead of displaying confidence. Regrettably, their actions cause colleagues to likewise doubt their abilities and question whether they are competent, thereby bringing their fears into reality.

If this leader instead masters their own internal voice to ensure it is healthy, positive, and beneficial, the success of managing their personal performance will engage others to connect with the goals they champion. It will inspire others to seek individual achievements for themselves. It potentially drives the communication levels of the entire organization around them upward and forward.

> *If this leader instead masters their own internal voice to ensure it is healthy, positive, and beneficial, the success of managing their personal performance will engage others to connect with the goals they champion.*

DE FEET OF FAILURE

Climbing the ladder to achieve success typically brings about a few casualties in the form of missteps, offenses, defeats, and failures. This reality gives even the best of us the opportunity to understand why negative chatter debilitates. We are human after all! The mistakes we make remain within our psyche and rattle, if only just a little, against the protective covering of our self-esteem. It takes a reasonable amount of pressure or, for some, only one chink in the precise spot, for a past slip-up to erode our carefully-constructed confidence and wreak havoc throughout the armor of perception we have of ourselves. Perhaps this is because there is work to do in the area of emotional intelligence to raise the threshold and develop resilience. Possibly critical awareness must be permitted to resolve past hurts and residual issues. Maybe there are relevant energies required towards visioneering, journaling, or scripting, for example, to dramatically facilitate propulsion of the mind, body, spirit, and emotions beyond the lingering event or circumstance. Perchance, alternative perspectives are best fully savored so hidden lessons are revealed.

As we move through life, on one plane or another, we may come face-to-face with one or more of these experiences, issues, persons, etc. that has caused harm. Effectively resolving hurt empowers us to move through its negative effects and purge it completely from our being.

The goal is to be open to new life experiences that bring joy, happiness, and positive outcomes. There is a wonderful outcome when we put forth intention with our whole being. I refer to the mind, body, spirit, and emotions, so there is work involved. Whether you realize it or not, harboring ill will, hurt feelings, bitterness, or unresolved pain aids in your undoing. Let me repeat that for those in the balcony... if you fail to resolve your wounds, whether great or small, those very wounds

218

will lead you to self-destruction. Choose whether harboring ill will or being open is most preferred.

Your job over the entirety of your lifetime is to ensure the aches of life are simply a lesson on the way to realizing your dreams. There are five steps you can take today to make this happen. If you find you require more extensive work, I encourage you to grab hold of someone who can support you being intentional with this process. These steps may seem simple; they are important to the process.

1. **DECIDE to Let Go.** Accept your decision in this moment to move past the issue. This means clearing your head every single time the episode repeats in your mind: breathing, jumping up and down, and/or performing some other physical activity, audibly stating affirmations with your emotions connected. Activate your decision and then consciously pursue acceptance of it in each moment.

2. **VENT the Experience.** After deciding to move past the pain, write a letter to get the memory of the hurt completely out of your system. Put every detail you remember down on paper. The goal here is twofold: to help you understand why you are holding on to the hurt and to help you see your responsibility in its occurrence. Wait a minute, hear me out! I am not saying you are fully accountable for what happened. We have all

either decided to actively create experiences that bring about our own desires in life or have decided to allow others to create experiences that we tolerate or accept. Either way! Consider taking ownership of how you could have better handled the situation, made a different decision, and even addressed your pain before now. Release the memory of the incident through your letter, as if you are speaking with a trusted friend who loves you dearly and is on your side.

3. **STEP into Your Power.** You, my friend, are not a victim! Your feelings matter, as well as your healing. It is vitally important that you begin to put your feelings in their proper perspective. Take time to understand what you feel and how it is driving you towards or away from your authentic being. Afterwards, decide to start feeling great, acknowledge why you feel great, how you feel great, and you will feel great! Feel invincible about your circumstances, about your experiences, about your life lessons. All your encounters have made you into the successful, incredible person that you are today! When you hold onto the negative residual matter, it robs you of who you could be apart from it. It means you hand your personal power to someone or something else. I encourage you to take charge today. Understand the emotions that plague you and why they have come. Then take back your power and create your joy.

4. **FOCUS.** After you have completed the letter exercise, fold it up, burn it, and let go! Cease and desist, let go. Since you are unable to change the past, embrace what you have today and make it the best ever! Choose what to think about, feel, and make happen. Bring everything you have, every sense, memory, awareness, and thought into the present. Find joy, peace, harmony, love, acceptance, and energy. Embrace the now. State this to help facilitate your acceptance, "I am wholly focused with every fiber of my being, my mind, body, spirit, emotions, and soul, on creating joy, peace, harmony, love, acceptance, and energy, all of which will launch me into my being me today." It is fully within your power to re-launch your ability to create the same power invested within you at birth. Decide today and then get on with it!

5. **FORGIVE.** Everybody deserves forgiveness, in one form or another. Resolve in your heart to move towards empathizing, seeing things from the other person's perspective, and attaching the hurt to the person's actions instead of dwelling on the person as bad. Forgiveness is vitally important because without it you stay stuck in the situation. This means the most important person you may forgive is you for allowing something and/or being stuck. Forgiving is a powerful action that has incredibly long-lasting benefits. Begin with, "I forgive (the person) for what you did, although it

hurt me," and continue with, "I forgive me for my part in allowing the situation and for continuing to beat myself up, not forgiving, not pushing past the incident, not letting it all go, and the like."

Good for you! Today you decided in a big way to release the pain of past hurts and step into your personal power to create joy and more fully realize your dreams. Congratulations!

FEEL TO DEAL

For some of us, we require additional work where it relates to our feelings. If you are unable to move forward after working thru the various exercises and action steps above, commit to more intentional emotional work. It will take time, energy, and further effort; once you become aware of what is required to cleanse and revitalize yourself, you will be empowered to stay on track. I encourage you to commit the time, energy, and effort, as well as the mental, physical, spiritual, and emotional involvement. Do whatever it takes! The best thing we can do for ourselves is to completely unravel, fall apart, and make space for the cleansing process.

Emotional unraveling involves the ability to acknowledge, process, accept, express, and then release the emotion in order to validate your feelings, understand them, and, possibly, communicate them to those who are important. This level of intimacy empowers you to respond to future experiences with new and creative ways. When you are ready, use the following for emotional cleansing.

1. **Acknowledge the feeling.** Recognize the truth that is revealed. Be honest with yourself regarding what you feel, how deeply you feel, what brought about the feeling, and where the feeling is resonating within. Give the feeling a name. To help you do this, use an emotional chart, such as The Feeling Circle originally developed by Dr. Gloria Willcox.

2. **Process the feeling.** Go to the exact place within yourself where the emotion is housed. This may be your head, your heart, stomach, back, etc. Sit there inquiring and exploring how deeply you are feeling, why you are feeling, and what brought the feeling about. Envision a safe space as you recall the circumstances. Seek to understand all you can from the experience. Welcome the details and depth of emotion that comes, however intense. Breathe through it.

3. **Understand the feeling.** Understand the meaning of the feeling in your reality. Recognize its consequence on your physical body. Identify the sensations that arise because of it. Pinpoint where in the body the feeling is held. Associate the ramifications the emotion may have upon your spiritual being. Know that this journey will empower your complete healing. You are safe!

4. **Express the feeling.** Touch the part of the body where the sensation is strongest and communicate your sentiment aloud. Continue for every area experiencing sensitivity. Acknowledge what you feel as you envision your pain and convey your emotions. To continue to progress through, consider writing what you are feeling in a private journal. Capture the experience initially from your own perspective, then write expressing your experience in the second person, you, and then use the third person, he/she. This allows you to progress through the ordeal moving it further and further away from you, until you release it totally.

5. **Release the feeling.** Now it is time to let all that you have been carrying go! Focus on the word you chose to identify your feeling. Visualize one area of the body where you have the feeling. While caressing this area, say aloud several times "I feel ---- here," using your word. Visualize the caressing removing that feeling, as a solid form. Fling the mass away from your body. Repeat this several times, especially if the feeling is in other areas. As you inhale, say aloud, "What I feel is my sole responsibility to process. How I receive and respond to emotional stimuli will now empower love, life, health, and beneficial significance for my body, mind, spirit, and soul! I am now completely empowered to resolve everything that comes my way." Repeat this as appropriate and hold its truth within your

consciousness for the next few moments, as you breathe freely. At every exhale, release the tension in your body until it totally subsides. You may choose to associate this with a word picture, song, aromatic smell, or activity such as a bath in your mind. As you create the healthy practice, go to the word picture and say the new word aloud, sing, smell, or engage in the activity. Now is the time to completely release the negative emotions. Imagine them blowing away in the wind. Congratulations!

This activity will take time and at the same time is worthwhile for removing stuck or blocked feelings that harbor unhealthy responses. Additionally, once you move past blockages, you will realize the power in engaging your emotions with your actions to magnify dramatic outcomes. Cleansing your being of overly-charged emotions creates the ideal frame of mind to combine purposeful actions with power and accomplish everything that you desire.

You have already been formed, equipped, and empowered with everything in the universe that you will ever want! You, my friend, have the most powerful arsenal already within you!

✓ Now that you fashion powerful self-talk...
✓ Now that you own and control your emotions...

225

✓ Now that you fully understand that every misstep prepared you for moments of triumph…

✓ Now that you understand why you must engage your emotions with believability and take immediate action…

It is your time!

Step out and claim every victory that is surely yours;
you are perfectly poised to prosper.

Know that you are an amazing creation! Already placed within you is the perfect arsenal to defeat every threat that dares to cross your path. Just as a fighter trains to utilize weapons for his triumph, so must you train. Become proficient with your power. Unleash your warrior and win!

> *Know that you are an amazing creation!*

ACTION WORKSHEET

To Nuke the Negative Self-Talk, *Chop the Chatter*:
1. Check It
2. Challenge It
3. Channel It
4. Change It

To Affirm Everything You Aim for:

1. Profess several declarations that validate each positive good thing on the list of channeled items.
2. Express the details of what you now strongly believe.
3. Assign the fullness of your emotion and believability.
4. Seal your beliefs with actions that validate your truths.

Express each declaration using the words 'I am' and 'I will' to affirm the certainty of the positive occurring.

To Release Your Past Hurts and Step into a Powerful Future:

1. Decide to Let Go
2. Vent the Experience
3. Step into Your Power
4. Focus
5. Forgive

To Unravel Your Emotional Blocks and Cleanse:

1. Acknowledge the feeling
2. Process the feeling
3. Understand the feeling
4. Express the feeling
5. Release the feeling

Congratulations! You just completed extraordinary work to remove every impediment from your path. At birth, you were equipped with incomparable greatness and are being perfected all along your journey. You are complete. Step forward. Go.

The world is waiting for you.

> *You are complete. Step forward. Go.*

Renee Hutcherson Lucier, CPC, is a speaker, author, trainer, and strategist. Renee brings over 30 years of diverse corporate experiences to her passionate pursuit of coaching. From engaging with others over the course of her entire life journey, Renee has a distinguished fervor that champions others in realizing victory.

Experiencing quite a number of challenges throughout her life, Renee has persevered while maintaining joy, exuding positive energy, developing hyper focus, and living present in each moment. She has developed an encouraging voice that speaks to the truth that all things are possible. Renee is a beacon of light to those looking for their own, using her ears, her heart, and her passion for others to find their true essence and live what they know to be true within their core being. Atlanta Creative Loafing's 20 People to Watch says, "Renee is an amazing mother, a fearless leader, a loving humanitarian, a brilliant person. She makes a most dynamic coach! You definitely want to hear her insight and be guided by her exceptional skill."

Renee is credentialed though the Center for Coaching Certification. She holds a Bachelor of Science degree in Business Administration Finance from DeVry University. She is the proud mother of one daughter, 23, and twin sons, 21.

THE WAY WE SPEAK MATTERS

Chārutā AhMaiua

INTRODUCTION

Have you ever wondered why people stay in toxic relationships much longer than they want? How about why smart people continue to work in companies they don't like or that have no upward mobility? Ever wanted to understand why so few people realize and live their passions? Still more curious is why we humans seem to struggle with transforming habits we know are not working for us over and over and over again? There are likely many complex causes as to why we have trouble moving from point A, where we are, to point B, where we want to be.

In this chapter, I propose we ultimately lack clarity and clear, decisive action in large part because of the limited way we speak about ourselves, others, and the world around us. Our use of language is directly related to our pathway for clarity. Our ability to be crystal clear and concise in our language is directly related to manifesting the lives we truly want. Thus, if we want to create and live a life we love, the way we speak matters!

Also in this chapter, I will share what I call limited language patterns, breaking them down into categories. In each category

231

I will use examples similar to ones I have heard my clients say over the years. Further, I will offer strategies to fellow coaches for how to gently guide clients away from limiting language patterns into what I call power language, offering possible examples without giving advice or leading.

Lastly, I will challenge some common, agreed upon uses of language, especially in the healing arts and health care professions, and categorize them as limited language patterns. I ask that the reader stay open minded, coachable, and experiment with the new way of speaking. I find that the shift from limited language patterns to power language is a subtle and profound one that takes some practice and getting used to, and it makes all the difference in the world!

> *...the shift from limited language patterns to power language is a subtle and profound one...*

LIMITING LANGUAGE PATTERNS VS. POWER LANGUAGE

Limiting Language Patterns, LLP, is a way of speaking about ourselves, others, and the world that by its very nature limits what is possible through negativity, confusion, or both. It can fragment us, deluding our power of manifestation and our ability to take responsibility for our own lives. It also limits others and the world around us, for it prevents us from perceiving people and the world around us accurately. Ultimately, it keeps us stuck and unable to intentionally author the lives we truly want.

Power Language, PL, on the other hand, is a direct, clear, and concise way of speaking that tells our brain exactly what it is we mean as succinctly as possible. It is either positive or neutral. When we use power language, we have a palpable, direct connection with the words we use, which powerfully assists us to create the reality we truly want.

LIMITING LANGUAGE PATTERNS

1: Using "You" When "I" is Meant

- "You know when you are feeling sad…"
- "When you are angry, it's hard to stay focused."
- "You think it is going to be one way and then it is not."

The above are examples I have heard clients say. They use the pronoun you when they are referring to themselves. This is an LLP because it deludes the individual by making it about another when in fact it is about themselves. Furthermore, it makes it difficult to access the actual experience directly. To solve my problems, I must experience them as mine.

Consider the first example, "you know when you are feeling sad…" If this client is indeed referring to themselves then we know the client is experiencing sadness; by using this statement instead of a direct I statement, the personal connection, access, and accountability to the sad feeling is unavailable to the client.

This way of speaking, subtle as it may be, makes it difficult to access the cause of the sad feeling, which could be significant.

To address this LLP with clients, I use Reflective Questioning. First, I listen attentively and then based on exactly what my client says, I offer a clarifying question. To the above example I may say, "You just said, 'You know when you are feeling sad,' what exactly do you mean here?" Typically, the client will say, "what I mean is, I am feeling sad." Then, depending on their response, I may ask, "How is that affecting you?" If the client continues to use you instead of I, either I continue to ask a similar question, or I may gently interject and share with them the power of using I when referring to oneself. It depends on the appropriateness and flow of the session. Using I statements can be scary at first because it demands ownership of one's experience. The effects are powerful.

2. Using Similes

- "It is like a stiff breeze could push me over."
- "I'm like a fireball of emotion."
- "I feel as happy as a clam."

While using similes can be poetic, when it comes to accessing clarity and focus to manifest the lives we truly want, sometimes they can be diluting and confusing. Using similes to describe how we are experiencing something is incredibly indirect and fails to say concisely what it is we are experiencing. It gives the brain an indirect, unclear idea of what is happening and the cause of it. This makes it challenging to take responsibility and transform it, if unwelcomed, or embrace it fully, if welcomed. Thus, it deludes our power of manifestation.

In the first example, what are they saying with, "it is like a stiff breeze could push me over"? When the second person says, "I'm like a fireball of emotion," what are they experiencing? When the third person says, "I feel as happy as a clam," what do they mean exactly? The answer is, I don't know, and chances are, the clients are also unclear. Thus, this way of speaking is confusing. As a coach, if I assume I understand what a simile means without asking for clarity, I could accidently and dangerously lead clients away from finding their clarity.

> *...if I assume I understand what a simile means without asking for clarity, I could accidently and dangerously lead clients away from finding their clarity.*

The most common use of a simile I hear from my clients again and again is the use of like before a feeling word. Consider the differences between the following examples:

- "I feel like I'm sad," versus "I feel sad."
- "I feel like he's so angry," versus "I feel he's so angry."
- "I feel like I'm too emotional," versus "I feel too emotional."
- "I feel like we are always fighting," versus "I feel we are always fighting."

235

The first LLP deludes the experience and disconnects the client from the direct, palpable feeling of sadness. The alternative PL directly connects the client to the feeling of what is being said, "I feel sad." Due to the direct, concise, alternate way of speaking, the client can then decide if what they are saying is accurate. If not, they can make a correction. The last statement, "I feel like we are always fighting," is likely inaccurate. If a client tells their brain again and again that they are always fighting, they are more likely to recreate the fighting or feel stuck in it. Instead, if they use the alternative PL, they create an opportunity to see the situation clearly as well as an opening to work with it as it occurs. This is power in action.

> *...they create an opportunity to see the situation clearly...*

To encourage direct, clear PL from my clients, I may simply state the simile back to them exactly as they said it and ask them for clarity. I may say, "what do you mean by 'it's like a stiff breeze could knock me over'?" A foundational aspect of Reflective Questioning is to keep the statement exactly as it was said because I trust that my clients understand what they are attempting to convey even if I am unclear. If I change their wording, even slightly, I could confuse them or change their train of thought. They could lose where they were and that could delay their process of finding answers or worse, lead them away from them completely. As a Reflective Questioning facilitator, my job is to get out of the way.

Every now and again, I will experience some pushback from clients such as, "but I just told you," and to that I often counter with, "if 5 people used that same simile, they might refer to 5 different things. I want to be sure I understand your meaning. Can you help me?" This gentle, humble language usually works to soften the exchange and continue with the coaching. If the similes persist, I often have my clients close their eyes and listen into the direct, PL way of speaking versus the LLP way they originally offered. That empowers them to directly experience the subtle and profound difference between the two and choose for themselves.

The incredible benefits of these slight adjustments are powerful. It gives clients an opportunity to refine their words, making sure they say what they mean. It also assists them to take responsibility for themselves and their feelings as accurately as possible. It is through this accuracy and clarity that confusion melts away and manifestation is possible.

I began coaching with my mentor Marianne Weidlein, creator of Reflective Questioning, back in 2007. I hired her because I wanted support in self-employment as a massage therapist. I had the talent and experience in the field and lacked discipline and business know-how. She assisted me to uncover the ways I undermined my success with LLP such as "I don't know the first thing about business," "I have not done massage therapy as long as so and so," and "I cannot stand to market myself in this materialistic world." Once I understood how the often judgmental language I used was affecting me and changed the way I thought and spoke about myself and others, attracting clients became easy. After 4 months of coaching, I quit my spa job, launched my private massage therapy practice, and had 40 percent of the clients I wanted, which was the exact amount of income I had made overworking as a fulltime massage therapist at the spa I had just left. It felt miraculous.

3: Miscellaneous Disempowered Language
- "I just want to become a doctor."
- "I'll try to be more disciplined with my eating."
- "I kind of like my job."
- "We fell into our old habit of fighting again."

This LLP category encompasses an incredibly broad and diverse use of disempowered language, including words such as: just, try, more, kind of, better, guess, fell into, etc.

What does "just" really mean? "I just want to become a doctor." Can you hear the subtle negation to their dream in that choice of language?

In the second example, the use of "try" is non-committal. When my client says, "I'll try to be more disciplined with my eating," what they are really telling their brain is something close to, "I might fail so I'll give myself an out by trying." This way of speaking lacks a firm resolve that they will indeed be successful and accountable in mastering their eating.

In the same example, the use of the word "more" further deludes their power. What is "more" saying? It brings the past right back into the present. If they are going to be "more" disciplined with their eating, it means they are going to be more than they were in the past. It implies the past was less than and lacks specificity. Instead of creating a clear, positive possibility independent of the past, they are taking the limitation of their past and bringing more of it into the present and the future. I say limitation of their past because their very use of language shows they were once undisciplined or less disciplined than they wanted to be with their eating.

What does "I kind of like my job," convey? If my client only "kind of" likes their job, what things don't they like about it? What are the reasons? If the reason for this coaching is about whether to stay in their current profession, then gaining clarity into these questions is critical. As a coach, I hear the LLP and ask for clarity. Perhaps the reasons for only "kind of" liking the job are changeable and they can stay in their profession happily with a few small adjustments. Perhaps the reasons for only "kind of" liking the job are indicators they are better served by moving on. Through asking clarifying, reflective questions these realities become clear.

In the last example in this category, how does a person "fall into" something? What does this mean? What power does it offer to my client for transformation? Using "fall into" takes the ownership out of the habit and makes it as happenstance as falling into a sinkhole. "Oh, it happened again!" If I ignored my clients use of limiting language in this way, I enable them to continue to feel victim to their negative habit of fighting again and again. To guide them into PL, I may gently ask, "what do you mean by fall into?" "How does this work?" "What are the reasons you continue to fight?" This elicits deeper reflection from my client and with that reflection, a real solution with a self-created action step is possible.

> *This elicits deeper reflection from my client*
> *and with that reflection, a real solution*
> *with a self-created action step is possible.*

4: Pieces and Parts, Spaces and Places Language
What do I mean by, "pieces and parts, spaces and places language?" Common examples are as follows:
- "A piece of me feels incredible compassion for her."
- "A part of me is so angry that we broke up."
- "I'm in a space of deep frustration."
- "I'm in a really uncomfortable place within myself."

This is by far the most common of all the LLP's that I encounter. To address this, I ask clarifying, direct, and reflective questions so that my clients gain clarity with each session. If this way of speaking persists, is abundantly used, and if I have a great deal of trust with the client, I may encourage language adjustments by asking them to listen to the phrasing with the original LLP and then with the PL alternative. I take it case by case.

The reason I am cautious about sharing this as an LLP with my clients and colleagues is because it is both an extremely common way of speaking in general and is also a readily reinforced way of speaking from the broader mental health care and spiritual communities at large. Questions such as, "what space you are in today?" or "what part of you feels like that?" are commonly asked by many professionals. I have heard or read well known people such as Oprah, Wayne Dryer, Katherine Woodward Thomas, and Barbara Max Hubbard use this LLP category as well as many personally known colleagues, friends, trained counselors, and psychotherapists. I will go so far as to say it is an expected way of speaking about complex and internal experiences in today's Western society.

My hypothesis is: 50 plus years ago, when the mental health professions like psychotherapy and counseling were gaining credibility and popularity, using this kind of language was a first step in supporting patients to evaluate and understand their internal experiences. Prior to it, perhaps people were cut off or shut down to self-awareness. Pieces and parts, spaces and places language are validating people's complex experiences to a certain point, and over time it distances people from their experience, making clarity difficult. Because using it is so popular today, the limitations of this way of speaking are almost entirely hidden from view. Let me illuminate this using the above examples.

What is this client saying when they use statements like the first, "a piece of me feels incredible compassion for her"? What piece? Or in the second example, what part of them is the part that experiences the anger when breaking up? A common possibility is that they are saying, "sometimes I feel" as in, "sometimes I feel compassion for her" or "sometimes I feel angry that we broke up." At other times, they may feel differently.

Sceptics may wonder about scrutinizing this way of speaking in the first place and to that I bring up the very premise of coaching philosophy, which is that we are already whole and complete.

If we truly feel whole, then we are served by language that reflects our wholeness. If I speak about myself in pieces and parts, I am using language that fragments or confuses me even further. This is also true with the spaces and places LLP.

"I'm in a space of deep frustration" puts the frustration somewhere other than an experience inside oneself. Where is that space of frustration actually? Speaking this way dilutes the client's experience of frustration. What the speaker is possibly saying is, "I feel deep frustration right now." Maybe a moment ago, they were feeling differently and that changed. It isn't a new space that is somewhere external, it is a new moment in time associated with a feeling. Using direct language that takes ownership of deep frustration gives the client access to understanding it and the power to manage the experience. If they continue to be in a space of deep frustration, they limit their ability to be free of it or at the very least see how their actions or inactions contribute to their frustration. This ultimately lacks power and makes transformation difficult.

> *Using direct language... gives the client access to understanding it and the power to manage the experience.*

At first glance, the last example of, "I'm in a really uncomfortable place within myself," seems appropriate and revealing. Diving deeper, what is the client saying here? Perhaps they are saying, "I feel really uncomfortable." I invite you to say both statements out loud to yourself right now: "I'm in a really uncomfortable place within myself" versus "I feel really uncomfortable."

You may notice a subtle and profound difference between the two. What I notice is that, "within myself" is unnecessary to say because "I feel" implies the experience is within. Also, I notice that the latter statement is connected to the true experience of the uncomfortableness whereas the former is slightly detached from it. Furthermore, the former statement implies there may be many fixed places within the speaker: a place of discomfort, happiness, sadness, etc., whereas the latter statement simply acknowledges a feeling and most closely represents the nature of feelings, which are fluid and changeable.

I invite you to say out loud the statements and their alternatives and see what you find. Experiment, have fun, and explore:

- "A piece of me feels incredible compassion for her," versus "sometimes I feel incredible compassion for her."
- "A part of me is so angry that we broke up" versus "sometimes I feel so angry that we broke up."
- "I'm in a space of deep frustration" versus "I feel deep frustration."

Saying it both ways is a strategy I use when a client is persistently using pieces and parts, spaces and places language. As coaches, it is important to use gentle, non-judgmental language. By having clients experiment they get to decide what works for them. My clients have consistently chosen to use the concise language after feeling into both versions.

Guiding clients to use direct and concise language might elicit discomfort, especially if the issues are sensitives ones. It is this very process of initial discomfort that creates the foundation for deep, authentic reflection and from this reflection, awareness of

244

the truth of the matter. In turn, the actions steps to transform the concern at the root/causal level are now available.

IN CONCLUSION

How important it is to refine our language and speech if we wish to create and live a life we love? Most of our clients are people who have accomplished many things in their lives, and still they desire coaching. What drives this? As I said earlier, I first hired a coach because I wanted to have a thriving massage therapy business. Then I explored deeper and to my surprise, I realized I lacked freedom, satisfaction, and self-expression in other areas of my life as well. I find this to be true with the accomplished people I work with; they often have a desire to take their lives to another level.

Learning how to be concise in our language, plus clear and direct in our speech, gives us the capacity to progress in unprecedented and profoundly rapid ways. We begin feeling the actual experience of wholeness, clarity, and decisiveness in our actions. We are powerfully responsible in our lives.

Paying such close attention to how we speak and think about ourselves, others, and the world around us gives us an ability to evaluate our words and determine if what we are saying and thinking is true. If not, we can adjust to accurately reflect our genuine experiences. This profoundly connects us to life by verbally taking a stand and giving voice to our truth. It provides power and ownership when tackling our blocks and limitations directly. Our language can help us let go of that which we do not want and bring what we do want into creation. What is left is an opening in which manifestation is born so creating a life we truly love becomes a true reality!

One of the most profound examples of this in my life was when I began speaking and thinking of my mother in a radically new way. From the age of 15 to about 27, I spoke of my childhood as if it was something done to me. I felt as though I was a victim and the difficult experiences I lived in my 20's was a direct result of my mother's treatment of me. I used language that reflected this narrative and kept it alive, such as "she abused me" long after the so-called abuse was over.

With the assistance of my amazing coach who gently illuminated my LLPs and facilitated my use of PL, over time, I was able to experience my mother completely differently and now we enjoy an authentic, loving relationship.

Instead of repeating the disempowering narrative of "she abused me," what I said instead, when questioned by my coach, were usually feeling statements. I said things like, "It hurt when that happened," "I felt disorientated," "I felt alone," "I felt incompetent." When I began using this direct and concise language to connect to these difficult experiences, I could finally begin to feel the painful feelings I avoided. Once I connected to those painful feelings and gave them presence and voice, there was an opening. In that opening, I experienced my past differently. I saw the fullness of my mother's life and her own challenges, independent of me. I finally saw her successes as well, which were unavailable in my original narrative. Lastly and most profoundly, I felt myself as the young person I was when the so-called abuse happened, being at times aloof and manipulative, taking pleasure in my mother's upset. This last realization was especially shocking and uncomfortable to feel because I had a different perception of myself. Although I was a child at the time, I had something extremely important to account for and in doing so I was free to create a new relationship with my mother. This level of radical honesty, reflected by my clear, concise language, was what set me on my pathway to be completely responsible for my life and thus, creator of my outcomes; all my outcomes.

Language mirrors and shapes consciousness; it provides a powerful bridge to either connect or disconnect us to life, to consciously or unconsciously create our life, and to express our innermost truth and purpose for being alive with or without power. Yes, the way we speak matters! What are you choosing for yourself? How are you empowering your clients? What are you and they ready for?

How are you empowering your clients?

Chārutā AhMaiua, CPC, BA is a Certified Professional Coach through the Center for Coaching Certification. Prior to receiving that training, she studied extensively with the late masterful coach Marianne Weidlein in her advanced coaching method known as Reflective Questioning.

Reflective Questioning changed Chārutā's life forever, first as a client and then as a student. After years of experiencing many different healing modalities such as yoga, meditation, dance, and traditional psychotherapy, she still failed to gain the permanent results she wanted. It was only after her own profound transformation with this powerful style of coaching that she decided to become a coach herself and then begin offering Reflective Questioning to clients in 2015.

Using this amazing technique, Chārutā guides individuals and professionals to the genesis of their concerns rapidly so they understand their unique blocks, transform them, and create authentic, self-expressed lives, which empowers clients to thrive.

Chārutā's is passionate about self-realization, self-employment, and starting a family; she is about to give birth to her first child. She feels humbled and blessed to be in such an incredible, dynamic, and evolving profession as coaching.

www.self-transformations.com

Made in the USA
San Bernardino, CA
06 January 2020